the Journey of a

MOTHER'S HEART

Encouragement for Moms

GLENDA MALMIN

Regal

A Division of Gospel Light
Ventura, California, U.S.A.

Published by Regal Books
A Division of Gospel Light
Ventura, California, U.S.A.
Printed in U.S.A.

Regal Books is a ministry of Gospel Light, an evangelical Christian publisher dedicated to serving the local church. We believe God's vision for Gospel Light is to provide church leaders with biblical, user-friendly materials that will help them evan-
gelize, disciple and minister to children, youth and families.

It is our prayer that this Regal book will help you discover biblical truth for your
own life and help you meet the needs of others. May God richly bless you.
*For a free catalog of resources from Regal Books/Gospel Light please call your Christian sup-
plier or contact us at 1-800-4-GOSPEL.*

Cover Design by Kevin Keller
Interior Design by Rob Williams
Edited by Deena Davis

LIBRARY OF CONGRESS CATALOGING-IN-PUBLICATION DATA
Malmin, Glenda, 1950-
    The journey of a mother's heart / Glenda Malmin.
    p. cm.
    Includes bibliographical references.
    ISBN 0-8307-2538-5
        1. Mothers—Religious life. 2. Motherhood—Biblical teaching. 3. Mary,
        Blessed Virgin, Saint—Motherhood. I. Title.

BV4529 .M34 1999
248.8'431—dc21   99-052689

1 2 3 4 5 6 7 8 9 10 11 12 13 14 15 16 17 18 19 20 / 05 04 03 02 01 00

Rights for publishing this book in other languages are contracted by Gospel Literature
International (GLINT). GLINT also provides technical help for the adaptation, transla-
tion and publishing of Bible study resources and books in scores of languages worldwide.
For further information, contact GLINT, P.O. Box 4060, Ontario, CA 91761-1003, U.S.A.
You may also send E-mail to Glintint@aol.com, or visit their website at www.glint.org.

I would like to dedicate this book to
my mother, Trevah Casson.
She nurtured me as a child,
trained me as a young woman
and released me as an adult to the
will and purposes of God
for my life. Thank you, Mom.
I will be forever grateful for
your unfaltering love and
unselfish devotion.

I would also like to dedicate this book
to all mothers, young and old.
A hearty thank-you to the mothers
of the Bible for blazing the trail and
setting examples for us to follow and
consider. A sincere salute to
contemporary mothers who are
nurturing, training and releasing
their children to "do whatever he tells
you" (John 2:5). May your "children
arise and call [you] blessed"
(Prov. 31:28).

CONTENTS

Section One
THE CALL TO MOTHERHOOD

Section Two
ENCOURAGEMENT FOR THE JOURNEY

Section Three
THE EARLY YEARS OF PREPARATION

Section Four

THE STAGES OF RELEASE

PREFACE

The journey of a mother's heart is unique to each woman, yet each journey also has threads of common experience—paths that feel both familiar and unknown. The journey converges upon moments of utmost hilarity and moments of dread. It contains fulfilled dreams and uncharted territories. It is personal and yet has the power to penetrate the heart of the next generation.

The motherhood journey has a beginning but no ending. Once you open yourself to it, your life becomes a continuum throughout the life of your child. The realization that you do not give birth to mere human flesh, but rather to an eternal soul, settles into your spirit in an awe-inspiring way.

Motherhood also has changing seasons. There will be days of joy, when you feel like there is no child quite like yours. And there will be days of frustration and exhaustion, when you are sure there is no child quite like yours. Through my own personal experiences as a mother and by observing the lives of other mothers, I have discovered that the seasons, as well as the emotions, of motherhood vary. I've also discovered that whether you are a single mom or a married mom, your journey has dimensions of commonality with all mothers.

These common threads also seem to be intricately interwoven with patterns I see in the life of Mary, the mother of Jesus. As I have studied her life throughout the years, I've been encouraged and refreshed by the challenges she experienced as a mother. She faced unique challenges, with a unique child.

I'd like for us to take a good look at her life throughout the following pages. I do not grant her any higher status than the Bible does, but neither do I feel that her life is less than a very significant example of motherhood. Her motherhood journey was, in fact, one that was challenged on every side. This ancient Mary was a mother much like most of us. She had questions, concerns, opinions and deep challenges. She was also inquisitive, contemplative and wise. I have found her life to be a heroic role model for positive, and very real, mothering.

Parenting is probably the biggest risk you will ever take in this life. Whether motherhood is your preference or not, if you are a mother, you have probably come to realize there is no one who can affect you the way your child can. Whether you have given up your child for adoption or adopted your child into your life, his or her very existence can affect you. Whether you planned your child or did not plan your child, he or she is a part of your personal life journey at the point of conception. Whether you like your children at this time or don't like them, their seasons of life will affect your season of life. To use an American sport broadcasting analogy, parenting tends to be either the thrill of victory or the agony of defeat.

One of the wisest things a mother can do is to walk this motherhood journey with someone—to look for examples along the way that will help her discover landmarks of wisdom to hold on to in times of storm. Mary's life is just such an example. Together, we will search out the pattern of her life as a mother and allow her example to shine a light on the journey of our own hearts.

I have placed a quoted portion of Scripture related to Mary at the beginning of each chapter. Then, in story and dialogue format, you will be introduced to her as though she were telling you a part of her story.

I have made no attempt to give you a hermeneutic interpretation of the quoted verses. Rather, I would like for you to apply to your own heart the lessons drawn from the biblical Mary's journey—as well as from some contemporary mothers' stories.

If you are unfamiliar with Scripture, I hope you will glean

much from the account of Mary's life. I think you will find this historical mother to be one with whom you can easily identify. Scripture reveals her to have been friendly, compassionate and caring. She was also inquisitive, sometimes a bit bossy, and yet truly humble and wise. You will read about the pinnacles of her mothering experience that left her so joyful she could do nothing short of bursting into song. You will also discover that her journey contained experiences so deep and sorrowful that any mother who has known sorrow will find solace in her life and in her wisdom.

This Mary was a mother much like you or the neighbor next door or the woman sitting near you at your workplace. The waters of her soul ran deep. As the fruit of her womb—her son—brought challenges to her personal journey, He also changed her life forever.

If you are familiar with Scripture, I hope you will take the time to read the account again and be freshly challenged by Mary's example. Resist the temptation to skip over the scriptural text. Read it once again and allow the account of this marvelous Mary to penetrate your life in a deep, significant and encouraging way.

I believe that as we look at the life of this extraordinary woman, we will discover a common bond with her. She had questions, concerns, opinions and deep challenges in her role as a mother. I haven't yet met a contemporary mother who cannot identify with each of these facets.

My greatest desire is that the reading of these pages will encourage you in the journey of your heart.

ACKNOWLEDGMENTS

I give honor and thanks to my Lord and Savior, Jesus Christ, for giving me salvation as a precious and personal gift. Thank You for leading and guiding me in my motherhood journey and for being a constant source of strength.

I would like to thank my husband, Ken, for his partnership in parenting and his faithfulness in marriage. Thank you for making me feel secure, not only as a wife but also as the mother of our children.

Acknowledgments and a very sincere thank-you to my two children, Ben and Angela. Without the two of you, the richness of my life experience would be greatly lacking. Your lives not only bring honor to your parents but to the Lord Jesus as well. I will be forever grateful for you both. Thank you for the journey; I'm glad our friendship will continue on into eternity.

I would also like to thank my personal prayer partners, Donna, Linda, Susan, Darla, Kelly, Detta, Donis, Andrea, Fred, Lynn, Robert and Donna. You are indeed testimonies of faithfulness and Christian partnership. Thank you for your prayers and constant encouragement. I pray that this book will honor the hours of prayer you have put into it.

THE CALL TO MOTHERHOOD

Chapter 1

HIGHLY FAVORED

In the sixth month, God sent the angel Gabriel to Nazareth, a town in Galilee, to a virgin pledged to be married to a man named Joseph, a descendant of David. The virgin's name was Mary. The angel went to her and said, "Greetings, you who are highly favored! The Lord is with you." Mary was greatly troubled at his words and wondered what kind of greeting this might be. But the angel said to her, "Do not be afraid, Mary, you have found favor with God. You will be with child and give birth to a son, and you are to give him the name Jesus. He will be great and will be called the Son of the Most High. The Lord God will give him the throne of his father David, and he will reign over the house of Jacob forever; his kingdom will never end."

LUKE 1:26-33

She was just a young teen living in a small town in the hills of the Lebanon range. The town was so small and insignificant that outsiders said, "Can anything good come out of that town?" Yet their rhetorical question did not affect her love for this place.

On a hillside just above the village she could sit and rehearse the history of her ancestors. It was a special place where she recounted the destiny of those who had gone before her and dreamed of the outworking of her own destiny.

If the town had any prominent citizens within its borders, she certainly was not one of them. She was just a common girl who lived in a common neighborhood. In fact, it wasn't long ago that she had stepped out of childhood into the dawn of her womanhood. Just an ordinary girl, even by her own admission, but she was brimming with life and soon to be married to the handsome carpenter down the street. Oh, how excited she was to be promised to him in marriage!

She also had a joy-filled relationship with her God. They met every day, and she poured out her heart to Him with abandon. He was more than a god to her; He was her Lord.

With God and her carpenter in her heart, how could she not rejoice!

History tells us her name was Mary. I wonder if one of her early morning chats with the Lord went something like this:

Here I am again, Lord. I'm here to have our daily chat. I worship You with all my heart and trust You completely. You know I do. But now, Lord, I have much to talk about. In just a few moments the hours of the day will begin to descend on me like the raindrops on my window . . . yes, yes, I know I can babble like a brook some days, but there's just so much—

What did You say? What's that? You want to talk with me today?
But Lord, I have so much on my mind—about the wedding and all.
Oh! You have something to say about that, too? What is it, Lord?

Wait a minute . . . who's that knocking on my door? Excuse
me, Lord.

Yes, sir? You have a message from the Lord for me? He says
I'm highly favored? Who, me? You're making me a little nervous
here. Yes, I know He's with me . . . He wants me to what? To
have a baby! Well, the Lord knows I want to . . . every young
bride does. All in due time, of course.

I have to admit I'm a little concerned about my abilities. I'm
not so sure I'll be a very good. . . . What? How could I possibly
have a bab—? Well, yes, I know at times I can be inquisitive
when I should be contemplative, but my mother always told me
this mothering thing is a big deal to God. You know, it's a high
calling as well as a privilege from the Father above.

How could I possibly . . . how could it be . . . after all, I'm so
young and inexperienced. Highly favored, you say? I'll have to
think about that one.

Can you remember the emotions you felt the first time you took
the pregnancy test and found you were actually going to be a
mother? If you are a mother, let me say to you what Mary was
told so many years ago: *You are highly favored!*

Whether you are like Mary—a young woman in her teens,
without a husband—or you are married, three decades older and
well along in the mothering journey, you are highly favored.
Whether you planned to have a child or didn't, if you do have a
child, you are highly favored.

If you've given your child up for adoption, you also have
been highly favored. It is an honor and a privilege just to carry a

child within your womb. In a society quick to do away with unborn children, you have honored God by giving life and opportunity to an eternal soul.

If you have adopted a child into your life, you have been highly favored as well. Even though you didn't bond with the child from within your body, your deep heart bond rings with a message of hope for life and promise throughout the generations.

To hear the call of motherhood is to hear the words of the ancient yet contemporary text of the Bible: "You are highly favored! The Lord is with you." It is the revelation of these words that will keep your feet on solid ground and encourage you when it seems there are no solutions. These words can open your eyes to the light of hope when darkness surrounds you.

The title of a book for pastors' wives, written by Gail MacDonald, seems so appropriate when it comes to mothers everywhere; that title is *High Call; High Privilege.* In God's eyes, that's what your call to motherhood is, regardless of your perspective or your circumstances.

To hear the call of motherhood is to hear the words of the ancient yet contemporary text of the Bible: "You are highly favored! The Lord is with you."

A STUNNING ANNOUNCEMENT

In the Jewish culture of Mary's day, marriage came about in three stages. The first stage was engagement, the second stage was betrothal, and the third was marriage.

The Jewish people believed that the decision to marry was too serious to be left to the dictates of the heart. Hence, parents would often arrange for their children to become engaged to one another with a future marriage in mind. This engagement was official but not binding.

The ratification of the engagement came several years later, making it official. This was known as a betrothal. The girls were generally in their early teens and the boys were a few years older. At this point, the girl had a choice about the marriage. However, once the betrothal was put into effect, it was legally binding; in other words, you were legally married but the marriage was not yet physically consummated. It was so binding, in fact, that it would take a document of divorce to break the contract. If the vow was broken during this period, it could be punishable with death by stoning. The betrothal usually lasted one year to allow the family to make wedding preparations.

With this in mind, most Bible scholars agree that Mary was probably about fourteen or fifteen years old at the time the angel came to visit her. Economically speaking, she was a lower-class maiden betrothed to an economically lower-class carpenter. She felt great surprise upon hearing the angel's greeting. In fact, Luke 1:29 says that she was "greatly troubled at his words." She had a realistic understanding of ranking in her society. Even though she was in the lineage of King David, she was still just a young maiden betrothed to someone who was not wealthy by any means.

When the angel went on to tell her the name and person of her son, she grew even more amazed. The angel said He would have the title of deity, "the Son of the Most High," and the title of humanity, "of his father David." When the angel said His "kingdom will never end," Mary's practical mind took over. Instead of dreaming about the prophetic cosmic greatness of her son and His kingdom, she wanted to know how this was going to happen.

Her question was not one of doubt, as Zechariah's had been six months prior to this. Zechariah had been praying for a child (see Luke 1:13). When his prayer was answered, he wanted another sign, something other than what the Lord had just provided him through the angelic visitation. So God gave him another sign—he took away Zechariah's ability to speak. Although God was still determined to bless Zechariah, this silence was a bit of a rebuke for seeking a further sign. The next time Zechariah was heard from in Scripture, he was speaking words of faith.

Mary, on the other hand, had not been praying about having a baby before her wedding. So when she asked her question about how this could be, she did not get a rebuke; she received an explanation. God does not seem to mind an inquisitive demeanor. In fact, I think He relishes our conversation and He loves to amaze us with His vision and purpose.

The messenger who spoke to Mary was Gabriel the angel. His name means "God is my hero." He was the same Gabriel whom God had sent to Daniel of the Old Testament to give him understanding when he needed it. (See Dan. 8:16,17; 9:22.) Isn't God good to send the right kind of messenger to us at the right time?

Gabriel told Mary, "The Holy Spirit will come upon you, and the power of the Most High will overshadow you" (Luke 1:35). This statement would have taken Mary's mind back to Exodus 40:34: "Then the cloud covered the Tent of Meeting, and the glory of the LORD filled the tabernacle." This glory that filled the Tabernacle was the same glory that would overshadow Mary and her child.

To build Mary's faith even more, Gabriel spoke of her cousin Elizabeth's miracle child. Elizabeth was in the midst of a similar circumstance. She was an anointed woman of God who would not only empathize with Mary's dilemma but would also identify and rejoice with her in it. What joy, what privilege to know a kindred spirit! God gave to Mary the gift of another woman to understand her and relate to her circumstances.

EMBRACING MOTHERHOOD

What was it like for you to hear the call to motherhood? Did you have anxious moments or months of waiting for the pronouncement that you were indeed expecting? Was it a time of joyful anticipation? That's how it is for many women.

Then the nausea begins. *Oh, how one remembers the nausea!* Other mothers tell you that you'll forget the labor pain and the nausea. *Don't believe it.* When you've raced to the toilet bowl yet one more time, it makes you seriously contemplate the arrogance of Eve and the stupidity of Adam in the garden. It's that nausea that causes you to look at brave, young expectant mothers with grace and mercy as you watch them turn green and run. Oh, yes, the blessings of motherhood far outweigh the nausea and labor pains, *but you don't forget.*

I can remember taking college courses during my first pregnancy. The classes were down the hall from the school cafeteria. As I entered the building, the aroma of breakfast still lingering in the air, I would promptly race to the bathroom, lose my breakfast and then go to class. Halfway through class I would excuse myself and kneel before the toilet once again. And yet once again by the time class was over. It became a daily routine.

Pregnancy provided some of the most memorable parts of my personal journey in life, toilet bowl and all. I prayed for, hoped for and longed for children; pregnancy was part of the experience. Have I forgotten it? Not on your life! Do I warn other young women who have yet to experience the blessings of pregnancy? Usually not. Do I laugh with (*with,* not *at*) those who are pregnant and turning shades of green as they run to the bathroom? Absolutely.

Granted, not every expectant mother's experience with pregnancy is the same as mine. Some sleep through their entire pregnancy (at least their husbands think so). They sleep late in the morning, early in the afternoon and on into the evening. Their pregnancy adventure is like a bear's hibernation pattern in winter.

Some women are seemingly unaffected by the nausea, labor pains or sleeping patterns. It's the baby in the rib section during the last month of pregnancy that brings surprising discomfort. Others skip and sing through the whole experience with nothing more than a slight frontal bump in their anatomy and a gentle rolling movement within.

Regardless of what your experience was or what it may be in the future, why not enjoy every phase of your life to the utmost? When you can look across the table at another friend who is also a mother and simply say, "Remember when . . . ?" and that's all it takes to make you both laugh hilariously, it's sheer delight!

Regardless of the nausea, the swollen ankles or the waddle in your walk, there's nothing you'll experience in life quite like the privilege of a life moving within your womb or snuggling in your warm embrace.

I will never forget the birth of my firstborn. At the mere writing of these words, tears spring to my eyes. When I looked at him for the first time, the feeling of awe, privilege and responsibility overcame me. I realized he was not just a desire—a yearning of nor an answered prayer; he was an eternal soul. What

st   thought! He was a soul I was now responsible for

bef   ord. A soul of whom the Lord was requiring me to be

a   d.

             elmed both with joy and anxiety—with the joy of

li   r of whether I was up to the task. I had a deep

             y need for the presence of the Lord to overshad-

             nd me as He had Mary.

penetrating emotions of utter need and utmost joy visited me again at the birth of my next child. Again I felt overwhelmed, humbled and exhilarated. I was shocked by the profundity of the responsibility with my first child and comforted by it at the birth of my second. There's nothing quite like utter dependence on God.

To know that God Himself is placing a gift of stewardship into your hands is both frightening and comforting. It makes you want to run and hide for fear of doing it all wrong. Yet it causes you to take comfort in the great trust He has placed in you. Your emotions all too clearly remind you of who you are and who He is; you are the created and He is the creator. He is the One you can depend on, and you are the one who needs Him at every turn.

If you are in the beginning stages of your motherhood, or somewhere in between, embrace and internalize the words Gabriel spoke to Mary so long ago. "Do not be afraid . . . you have found favor with God. . . . The Holy Spirit will come upon you, and the power of the Most High will overshadow you" (Luke 1:30,35).

Chapter 2

ACCEPTING THE CHALLENGE

The angel [said], "For nothing is impossible with God."
"I am the Lord's servant," Mary answered. "May it be to me
as you have said." Then the angel left her.

LUKE 1:35,37,38

Mary is amazed and a little troubled by what God's messenger has told her about her son and who He will be. Then the angel tells her about the miracle involving her relative Elizabeth and proclaims, "For nothing is impossible with God."

In all the stories Mary has ever heard about the great "I Am," she has never heard those specific words spoken to anyone. Why did the messenger say this and what should her response be?

"For nothing is impossible with God." That's what he said. Oh, my mind is awhirl with a million thoughts! And yet there is but one thought at the forefront—the revelation of who I am and who my God is. Has there not always been a joyful anticipation of the future deep within my heart? Yes, yes, it's all true!

I am the Lord's servant. That's it; I am the Lord's servant; not my mother's or Joseph's but the Lord's. Yes, Lord, let it be to me as You have said. I trust You, Lord, and I anticipate the future with joy. Let it be to me as You have said.

My heart and mind are so full.

Where did he go? The messenger . . . he's gone . . . what to do, what to do...

Can you remember feeling overwhelmed, underwhelmed and every emotion in between at the news that you were expecting? You laughed, you cried, and you jumped up and down. You phoned long distance, short distance and any distance to spread the good news. You felt empowered, overpowered and underpowered all at once.

One minute you were in the doctor's office, feeling exhilarated and secure. The next minute the doctor had disappeared. As you got up from the examination table, all of a sudden it hit you: *I'm going to be a mother! Is it really true?*

In the various stages of mother-hood—from pregnancy to the young adult years of your child's life—did anyone ever say to you, "You'll make it; you'll do fine, dear"? Was your response, at least in your head, *I can't do this! I don't know the first thing about mothering! It's great for you to think that, but you just don't know!*

Did the enemy of your soul ever come and whisper in your ear, "You didn't even like taking care of your siblings; how could you be a mother?" Have you ever felt totally unworthy of receiving that heart-felt Mother's Day card?

The enemy loves to take the generalizations of well-intentioned encouragement or the whispers from his own darkness and cause us to forget that it is the Lord who has called us to motherhood; it is Him we serve. Satan loves to get us focused on status and comparison rather than on our role and God's abilities.

Even if you were an only child and never took care of another child even once in your growing-up years, you can still be a good moth-er. The Lord wants to say to you, as the angel Gabriel said to Mary long

You may have questions about your skills and abilities as a mother; but the Lord will help you, for nothing is impossible for Him.

ago, "Nothing is impossible with God." Remember, Gabriel was the angel who came to give understanding to Mary, and the message that God can do anything was the understanding God wanted him to leave with Mary.

You may have many questions about your skills and abilities as a mother. But the message the Lord wants you to hear today is that He will help you, for nothing is impossible for Him.

NOTHING IS IMPOSSIBLE WITH GOD

When the angel Gabriel spoke to Mary, the word "impossible" had never before been recorded in any of the ancient manuscripts of her people. In fact, the word "possible" had not been written until Jesus spoke the word "possible" for the first time in a discussion with His disciples about who could be saved. His response? "With God all things are possible" (Matt. 19:26).

This message had been woven carefully throughout the fabric of ancient history. From the creation of Adam and Eve to the rebuilding of the walls of Jerusalem in the book of Nehemiah, everyone knew that all things were possible to a people who were willing to believe and follow Jehovah. However, when the angel spoke to Mary, Jehovah had not been heard from for 400 years—not since Malachi's time.

For a messenger such as Gabriel to show up and proclaim in such specific terms that "nothing is impossible with God" must have been quite a thought-provoking revelation. To have an angelic visitation was one thing, but to have him sum up the cornerstone message of history in such a succinct manner must have been earthshaking to young Mary. Not only was his proclamation a summation of God's perspective on history, it was also a personalized message to this humble teen concerning her life and the life of her child.

Mary would need this message engraved on her heart to survive the difficult things in the years to come. Not only would her child be unique, but her personal reputation would be brought into question as well, and her life would be affected forever. Could she do all that the Lord was asking of her? She was a simple young girl with a simple desire to serve the Lord in her generation. She didn't have any extraordinary dreams or desires that went beyond what the will of God was. He would take her simplicity and humility and show the world what He could do with a yielded heart.

HALLMARKS OF MARY'S FAITH

In Luke 1:5,6, we meet Zechariah and Elizabeth. Luke devotes considerable attention to issues of status, characterizing both of them as upright and blameless. He strategically notes their location in the Temple, which is the central point of Jewish focus. Luke also notes that Zechariah had chosen the lot to be the celebrant priest for the week. He had been honored to do the sacred function of burning incense. This was the most solemn part of the day's service in the Temple. It symbolized that God accepted Israel's prayers of repentance. It was considered the highest mediatory act a priest could do for his fellowman.

From the Temple in Jerusalem, Luke takes us to small-town Nazareth and a young girl betrothed to a common carpenter. Mary's betrothed, Joseph, is a "son of David," but he and Mary are not married yet, so Mary has no current claims on his inherited status. Luke tells us later that Mary is the relative of Elizabeth. This should have given her the status of being in the priestly line. However, it doesn't give her much status from a Jewish perspective, which considered hereditary purity as passed down through the male. Mary's insignificance seems to be Luke's primary point in his introduction of her here.

In the Greco-Roman world, and in Judaism, the very status of a slave was determined by the status of its householder. So when Mary responds, "I am the Lord's servant," she is acknowledging that her status comes from her relationship with God rather than from Joseph her betrothed or Elizabeth her cousin.

From this point in Scripture, we see a status reversal. Mary moves from being a lowly handmaiden to one worthy of acknowledgment. Throughout Jewish history, proper greetings always were spoken from the younger and less significant to the older and more significant. The man also was considered to be more significant than the woman and was greeted first. This hierarchy of significance seems to have changed for Mary at this point in the text.

In Luke 2:5, Luke notes that Joseph went "to register with Mary." In verse 16, Mary's name is mentioned before Joseph's. We also see that Simeon, in verses 33 and 34, "blessed them and said to Mary." Rather than addressing himself to Joseph, the supposed father, Simeon addressed them both and then focused specifically on Mary. In verse 48 of this same chapter, we see Mary speaking for herself rather than waiting for Joseph to take the lead in the conversation.

This is a huge jump for Luke to make when, at the outset of the book, he went to such effort to emphasize the importance of status. This is just one aspect of how we see God fulfilling His words that "nothing is impossible with God." Even social status can be uprooted and turned around when God is involved.

I am not implying that women are any more significant to God than men are. I am merely stating that Mary exemplifies the importance of each individual deriving his or her status from the Lord and not from others. Mary's revelation of the sovereignty and strength of her God—and her humble posture that allowed Him to do with her and her son what He designed—would carry her through every phase of motherhood. Those two acknowledgments—who God was and who she was—were the hallmarks of her faith.

A SONG OF FAITH

I have a friend who received a similar awareness of God's ability to pour out grace for seeming impossibilities. Her awareness didn't come in the form of an angelic visitation but in the form of a baby boy who was severely handicapped from birth.

My friend was, and still is, a firebrand for the Lord and His purposes. Like Mary, she had no desire short of serving God in her generation. Unlike Mary, she was more than betrothed; she was married. She and her husband had started their journey together with joy and anticipation of all God had planned for them. They were a vibrant young couple excited with life and totally yielded to His purposes. They anticipated the birth of their first child with great joy.

When the baby was born, he was diagnosed as severely retarded and terminally ill. He was totally paralyzed, blind and deaf, and had what doctors termed failure to grow. He had increasing seizures and was only able to eat through a tube in his stomach.

The doctors wanted to medicate him but not feed him. They didn't see his value. They didn't know that he was the firstborn of three brothers yet to come. They didn't know how he would stretch and increase the faith of his parents for the future as well as the present. They didn't know how his very life would be as a golden thread woven into the fabric of the lives of those who would love him and snuggle him close to their hearts.

Basically, the doctors simply didn't realize who his creator was: "Who gave man his mouth? Who makes him deaf or mute?

Who gives him sight or makes him blind? Is it not I, the LORD?" (Exod. 4:11). They didn't realize who would so carefully watch over this baby. "See, I have engraved you on the palms of my hands; your walls are ever before me" (Isa. 49:16).

The doctors predicted a dirge of misery for this mother and death for her son. However, it wasn't a dirge that found melody in her heart. It was a sweet song of faith. Perhaps her son would not be like other boys his age. Perhaps he would not have long life, but he had life. That's what this mother chose to delight in. She refused to let the pathway of sorrow plague her. Although it met her at turns in the road, she chose the pathway of the "possibles" and handled the "impossibles" as they came along.

As it was with Mary, this young mother experienced God's all-encompassing grace as she yielded to His will each day. As it was with Mary, she too needed insight and courage from the Father for what lay ahead. This portion of her journey would also be the hallmark of her faith.

This firstborn son died when he was 18 months old. His life was brief, but it was precious and stirred faith and courage in the hearts of all who drew near to him. He engraved a blessing on his mother's heart and caused showers of grace to saturate her very soul. One of her sustaining Scriptures in this season was 2 Corinthians 12:9: "My grace is sufficient for you, for my power is made perfect in weakness."

At the birth and death of this very special firstborn son, my friend's heart was forever woven with Mary's. Somewhere in the heavens some divine stirring must have taken place each day as she bowed her knee and beckoned gentle whispers from the Lord. She must have listened closely for the reminder that "nothing is impossible with God" and that His grace would be sufficient for her. Then, just as Mary had done long ago, she humbly acknowledged in her spirit, "I am the Lord's servant. May it be to me as you have said."

This mother's heart was tuned to the impossibles turning into possibles. The doctors recommended that she never have another child. They warned that the risk of having another baby with similar handicaps loomed large on the horizon. This mothering adventure had now become more than a brief trek through an unknown land. It had become the pilgrimage of a brave pioneer willing to forge ahead.

At the writing of this book, my friend has one son in heaven and three vibrant, healthy, growing sons who love Jesus. She and her husband continue to walk in steadfast faith and commitment to the Lord and His purposes.

ARRIVING AT AN UNPLANNED DESTINATION

Parents in this or a similar situation often describe it like a planned journey that goes awry. It's as though you spend months preparing for a trip halfway round the world. You save money to purchase your airfare. You read books, watch videos and listen to lectures about the land you are going to visit. You even exercise in preparation for the trip because you know that when you arrive, there will be some mountains to climb and forest trails to hike. You're not afraid of those treks; they're part of what makes the land unique and inviting. You look forward to the challenge before you.

The day comes when you board the plane. You're prepared with knowledge, dreams and well-marked maps in hand. The flight goes fine and the long-awaited touchdown of the plane on the concourse is exhilarating. But as you step off the plane, a sinking feeling sweeps over your soul. Rather than tropical breezes and lush green forests, snow-capped mountains and blizzard conditions greet you.

Nothing you've thought about or brought with you has prepared you for this location. Neither the videos nor the classes have prepared you for this land. Maps of hiking trails and the lightweight clothing in your travel bag will do you little good. This is simply not your planned destination.

It's interesting to note that after the angel made his proclamation to Mary concerning the impossibles and she said okay, Scripture simply says, "Then the angel left her." It doesn't say that God left her, but it does say that the messenger who came to impart understanding left her.

Have you ever felt like you've just arrived at an unplanned destination you're totally unprepared for? You finally muster up the courage to ask some reasonably intelligent questions and you can't seem to find a knowledgeable person around to ask. In fact, there doesn't even seem to be a person in sight with a sane or compassionate perspective.

Do you remember what you felt like when you first looked at your child and thought, *I've met my match.* You cried out, "Lord, I am incapable of handling this child another day!"

Was it when your child looked at you mischievously just as he was about to put his little finger in a nearby electrical outlet? Was it when the doctor came and told you that your child had a heart defect? Was it when you had to leave your groceries unchecked in the market and chase your child down yet one more aisle? What did you do with that newly discovered feeling of dismay? In that moment, did you identify with Mary? I can tell you that she could identify with you.

Whether your child is severely handicapped, has an attention deficit disorder or a reading disorder, or is simply in an annoying or rebellious phase, there are times when you may need to cling to the proclamation, "Nothing is impossible with God." There will be times in your mothering when you've reached that unplanned destination. Your help will not come through your lineage, your identification with your marriage partner or a parenting class. Though you'll reach out desperately for an explanation, you will discover your answer is in a simple proclamation of faith and a yielded heart to the God who designed the journey.

RISE TO THE CHALLENGE

In Mary, we see that God gave His favor to a person who by all cultural standards measured low in status due to her age, family heritage and gender. She humbly received favor from God, wisely discovered her identity by yielding to His perspective and will for her life and bravely accepted the challenge. He raised her from a position of lowliness by choosing her and equipping her to have a central role in His plan of redemption for the human race.

We, too, must derive our status from our relationship with the Lord. Regardless of what challenges we face, we can stand in the knowledge of who He is, not what we are capable of. We, too, can yield to His call and rise to the challenge He presents to us.

After the angelic proclamation, "Nothing is impossible with God," Mary simply said, "All right, Lord. I am your servant. Now fulfill all that You have destined for me and my child."

Whether you feel up to the challenge or not, grasp hold of Gabriel's proclamation that with God nothing is impossible for you, your child and the journey of your heart. Acknowledge that you are the Lord's servant and surrender to the Lord by telling Him, "May it be to me as you have said." And when those who would be capable of bringing understanding to you are far from your side, you will also see that His grace is sufficient for your needs.

Section Two

ENCOURAGEMENT
FOR THE JOURNEY

Chapter 3

THE OTHER VOICES

The Lord is with you.

LUKE 1:28

*At that time Mary got ready and hurried to a town in the hill country of
Judea, where she entered Zechariah's home and greeted Elizabeth.*

LUKE 1:39,40

*This is how the birth of Jesus Christ came about: His mother Mary was
pledged to be married to Joseph, but before they came together,
she was found to be with child through the Holy Spirit. Because Joseph
her husband was a righteous man and did not want to expose her to public
disgrace, he had in mind to divorce her quietly.
But after he had considered this, an angel of the Lord appeared to him in a
dream and said, "Joseph son of David, do not be afraid to take Mary home as
your wife, because what is conceived in her is from the Holy Spirit.
She will give birth to a son, and you are to give him the name Jesus,
because he will save his people from their sins."
All this took place to fulfill what the Lord had said through the prophet:
"The virgin will be with child and will give birth to a son, and they will
call him Immanuel"—which means, "God with us."
When Joseph woke up, he did what the angel of the Lord had commanded him
and took Mary home as his wife. But he had no union with her until she gave
birth to a son. And he gave him the name Jesus.*

MATTHEW 1:18-25

W hat a journey Mary had committed herself to! The messenger from God had deeply imparted to her the understanding that the Lord was with her, and her response was, *Okay, let it happen.* Then the messenger simply left.

Was this scene just a figment of her imagination? Now where could she go for a confirmation that her experience was reality and not just some wild imagining? On one hand she felt excited; on the other she felt desperate. She needed confirmation and perspective. She needed people. Where were the others who would walk this journey with her?

Then Mary remembered that the angel had mentioned her cousin Elizabeth. That's it! She would go to Elizabeth! Even though the distance from Nazareth to the hill country of Judea was almost a hundred miles, her heart had begun a journey, and now her feet must join in.

But what about Joseph? Even though she was courageous enough to ask her questions boldly and not be intimidated by the angel, what about Joseph? For now, she must be wise enough to hold her tongue. She must let God speak for her. After all, Joseph was a righteous man who wanted to do right by God. Surely God would speak to him. Now she must go to Elizabeth.

I wonder if her personal "ponderings" and conversation with God on that day went something like this:

"May it be to me as you have said." What was I saying? And where did Gabriel go? Maybe this wasn't real. No, I'm not given to figments!

Okay, heart, calm down. Just think about what he said. "Don't be afraid . . . you are favored by God...your son will be great . . . the Holy Spirit will come on you . . . Elizabeth is going to have a child... nothing is impossible."

Oh! Elizabeth is going to have a child!

How can this be? It must be the "nothing is impossible" thing. Elizabeth . . . that's it! She's my confirmation. If God has favored her with a miracle, then maybe that really was Gabriel with God's message for me. Maybe it's true that nothing is impossible. Yes, I believe it is. O God, do let it be to me and mine as You desire. I do want to do Your bidding.

And thank You, God, for the others. You know how I need them in my life. Thank You for Your messenger Gabriel and for Joseph and Elizabeth. Even though Elizabeth is almost a hundred miles away, I'm on my way to see her.

Sorry, Lord, for being the babbling brook that I am. You are so good to me, and I just love You so. Okay, I'm off to see Elizabeth. What will she say when I arrive? What will she think of me? O God, do go before me!

And God . . . what about Joseph? You know how much he wants to please You. He's known as a righteous man in the neighborhood. What will this do to him, to his reputation? Yes, Lord; I trust You. Okay, I'm on the trail to Lizzie's house; we'll talk about Joseph later.

FINDING YOUR "ELIZABETH"

Can you remember moments in your mothering journey when you felt alone and desperately needed other people in your life? Did you ever attend a women's conference on parenting and feel like you were the only one in the room who was sinking lower and lower in your chair as the speaker gave a discourse on proper parenting?

Remember all the speakers who told you that if you did certain things you would get certain results with your children? Do you remember attempting to do all those things down to the letter and getting results that didn't look anything like what they had described?

As a young mother, I can remember sitting in a conference and listening intently to the speaker talk about parenting. She was inspiring and articulate. It seemed that everything she said, I was doing. As she spoke, I reflected that my toddler was active and busy but definitely responsive to my intuitive parenting skills. I was feeling pretty good about myself.

Not long after the teaching session, the speaker sought me out. She began to apologize for using me as a negative illustration in her session. I was shocked! I had not heard my name mentioned, and I couldn't see myself in any of her negative illustrations of how not to parent.

Nevertheless, there she was, admitting that one of the primary illustrations of how not to do it was most definitely me. Admittedly, it was based on only one observation of me and my child during one church service, but it was still an observation that she had shouted from the rooftops, so to speak.

The only reason she came to me was because I had attended the session and she was sure I was offended by her use of me as an example. Well, she was mistaken. I hadn't been offended because I hadn't recognized me. Now I was offended. I felt shock, dismay and embarrassment. After all, I had been feeling pretty good about my child and myself. I was delighted about our potential as a mother-child team.

Neither my mother nor my mother-in-law were geographically close at hand to give me advice on this part of my parenting journey. However, I sincerely thought I was doing okay. Now, to realize that someone I respected had a word of impending disaster for me rather than encouragement was frightening. I suddenly felt very alone in my mothering journey. I felt desperate for a mentor who would encourage me rather than judge me. I soon began to seek out some women to give me perspective and hope.

We all need others to come alongside us from time to time. We need those who will encourage us in our motherhood, regardless of the season we're in. We need others who will hear and speak the Word of God to us but do so in kindness.

If you've received harsh or alarming predictions about your parenting early in your journey, don't close yourself off. Whatever you do, stay open to the perspectives and input of others. Don't miss discovering the sensitive encouragers while you're attempting to dodge the insensitive ones. As Titus says, let the older women "train the younger women to love their husbands and children" (Titus 2:4). From the outset of your motherhood journey, surround yourself with encouragers.

We all need others to come alongside us from time to time. From the outset of your motherhood journey, surround yourself with encouragers.

THE LORD'S ENCOURAGING VOICE

The Lord's voice was the first voice that came to Mary through His messenger. Gabriel told her, "The Lord is with you" (Luke 1:28). This is a key insight for all mothers. I can only imagine that among Mary's many ponderings, this one was at the top of her list.

It wasn't only Joseph or Elizabeth who would be there to encourage her. It wasn't just the neighbors she had grown up with or her husband's future clientele. It wasn't even the local rabbi or her own extended family that would guide her on a daily basis. *It was the Lord.*

Mary must have meditated on what Solomon had written so long ago: "He who fears the LORD has a secure fortress, and for his children it will be a refuge" (Prov. 14:26). How comforting that revelation must have been. The God she loved was with her and would always be a refuge for her.

And so it is with contemporary mothers. No one can be with you and your children every waking moment except the Lord. The prophet Isaiah promises, "He gently leads those that have young" (Isa. 40:11). The psalmist also promises,

> He will not let your foot slip—he who watches over you will not slumber; indeed, he who watches over Israel will neither slumber nor sleep. The LORD watches over you— the LORD is your shade at your right hand; the sun will not harm you by day, nor the moon by night. The LORD will keep you from all harm—he will watch over your life; the LORD will watch over your coming and going both now and forevermore (Ps. 121:3-8).

A portion of a song titled "Trust His Heart" says it this way:

For He sees the first and the last
And like a tapestry,
He's leading you and me to someday be just like Him.
God is too wise to be mistaken

God is too good to be unkind
So when you don't understand
When you can't see His plan
When you can't trace His hand, trust His heart.

He alone is faithful and true.
He alone knows what is best for you.
So when you don't understand
When you can't see His plan
When you can't trace His hand, trust His heart.[1]

Isn't it amazing to realize that the God of the universe is always watching over you and your child?

ELIZABETH'S ENCOURAGING VOICE

When I look at Elizabeth, I see a godly, warm kindred spirit who was just what the young Mary needed. Elizabeth was wise and full of grace. She was rich in heritage, a descendant of Aaron and married to Zechariah, a priest who was also a descendant of Aaron.

A son born to Zechariah and Elizabeth would have been entitled to a place of employment among the priests. The double lineage represented huge blessings and priestly rights to their offspring. It also afforded them great respect in the community as a married couple.

However, because the Jewish priesthood was solely based on family descent, and Elizabeth was barren, their marriage was looked upon with sorrow and grief; and her barrenness was considered a disgrace.

At that time, most Jews concluded that if you were barren, you must have some secret sin that God was judging. Jewish rabbis proclaimed there were seven people who were excommunicated from God. The list began with "a Jew who has no wife, or a Jew who has a wife and who has no child." Barrenness was even considered grounds for divorce.

But to God, barrenness was not considered a reproach. Although children are a blessing from God, they are not necessarily a sign of His supernatural blessing. God loves each individual, whether that person is single or married, childless or with a "quiver full" (Ps. 127:5).

Elizabeth and Zechariah had not known or understood God's reasons for their childlessness, but they trusted in His sovereignty. They hadn't known they were waiting to be the parents of the forerunner of the promised Christ. They hadn't known how detailed God's timing was in their lives and in the life of their child. All they knew was that they trusted God. He would be on time with the answer, and He would bless them and their seed beyond that which they could imagine in their present circumstances. So they waited and trusted.

Elizabeth had known the effect of being in the priestly line for better and for worse. She had known pride and joy in her marriage to Zechariah and she had known shame and rejection in her barrenness. Perhaps part of the reason for the timing in Elizabeth's motherhood journey was to allow her to be a mentor to the young mother who would one day be on her doorstep. She who was familiar with shame and rejection would know how to infuse her young disciple with faith for the future and joy in the present.

It was a new day, and Elizabeth, like Mary, had experienced a miracle. She, too, had a special child within her womb. She had learned how to ride disappointment in a direction toward the Lord rather than away from Him, and He had blessed her. Together, she and Zechariah had contended in prayer for a child.

They never abandoned their faith in God. They held strongly to the belief that the impossibles could become possibles.

The only way for Mary to check out the angel's word to her was to check on Elizabeth. This was not unbelief but wisdom. She needed someone other than her own ears and perceptions to affirm God's Word to her. God had given her the hint; why not move on it? It was the same principle Paul would teach in 1 Thessalonians 5:21: "Test everything. Hold on to the good."

The day came when Mary arrived from Nazareth to the hill country of Judea. It was common for the door of Jewish homes to be open during the day, and guests would step inside and express a greeting to the householder who would then respond.

In Luke 1:40 we see that Mary entered the house and called out a greeting to Elizabeth. The next verse notes that as soon as Elizabeth heard the greeting, the baby leaped within her womb and she was filled with the Holy Spirit. In a loud voice she began prophesying to Mary about her blessing.

Not only is this a confirmation to Mary, but it is a prophetic fulfillment to Elizabeth as well. The angel of the Lord who appeared to Zechariah in the Temple told him that John would "be filled with the Holy Spirit, while yet in his mother's womb" (Luke 1:15, *NASB*).

God will place Elizabeths in your life for your encouragement. To find them you may have to make a long-distance call, volunteer to help at an event where other mothers are, or talk with the grandmother next door. These women may or may not be genetically related to you. They may be young or old and they may come in all shapes and sizes.

You'll need them from time to time, and in some seasons you'll need them every day. Often, they will show up when you least expect them, in unplanned places. Look and listen for encouragers; they're often just an arm's reach away.

INFORMAL MENTORING

Is it possible to balance our busy contemporary lives with our mothering? Is it possible to give love and service with abandon to both the harvest field and our own children? When questions like this assail you, that's when you need an Elizabeth to step into your life.

Though still in her twenties, Sharon and her husband, Bob, were veterans to the mission field. She had grown up in Africa, and she and her husband had ministered there a few years together. Now they were in Taiwan, a new land to both of them. This assignment presented Sharon with new and unique challenges. Not only did she need to minister to her husband and those around her, but she also had to learn a new language and balance her daily responsibilities. She was a mother of two active children, ages six and four, and she was also a missionary. What fulfillment she felt, what joy reigned in her heart!

She loved her husband, her children and her calling. Her heart was joined not only to the African people and those of her homeland but to the Taiwanese people as well. She delighted in these challenges. However, by her own admission, she sometimes was frustrated by her perfectionistic tendencies to do everything well.

Sharon had an administrative bent and loved for things to run according to plan. This asset could sometimes become a hindrance. Sometimes it robbed her of discovering the joy in the moment. Unplanned circumstances could shift her focus from people to frustrated plans. If there's one thing every successful missionary knows, it is that even the best-made plans do not always go according to design. Every mother needs to realize this as well. The administration of plans is a blessing but not quintessential.

Jesus came to die for people, not for schedules and ideal situations. In fact, there is no recorded time when Jesus actually prayed for plans and schedules, but He often prayed for people. When the time came that Sharon's in-laws were coming for a visit, she looked forward to it expectantly and wanted everything to go well. She was especially excited that they would be there to celebrate her son's sixth birthday. She had planned a special party for him and his friends.

While Sharon was busy with the details of the party, she noticed her mother-in-law playing games with the children and singing songs with them. That day her mother-in-law's actions demonstrated the message: Enjoy your kids. Sharon felt a surge of gratitude for this example.

One day during her in-laws' visit, they all went to Sun Moon Lake. This was a special place of beauty in Taiwan. They planned a boat ride on the lake and Sharon prepared a nice picnic lunch.

As they approached Sun Moon Lake, it began to rain. Determined to fulfill the plan of the day, they boarded the boat for a ride on the lake and were literally drenched by the rainfall. Sharon felt both deprived and denied; to put it plainly, she was grumpy.

They found a place near the lake with a small roof over it. With a cloud in her heart as well as over her head, Sharon began to organize the picnic lunch. Suddenly her mother-in-law jumped up from the table and challenged the six-year-old to run and catch her. They did this until everyone joined in the fun. Once again Sharon received a message from her mother-in-law's example: Make the best of it regardless of the circumstances.

A Danish proverb says: Who takes the child by the hand, takes the mother by the heart.[2] The message of Sharon's Elizabeth, spoken not in words but in gracious deeds, engraved a memory in Sharon's heart for the years to come.

It was at Sun Moon Lake in Taiwan, that rain-drenched day, that the hearts of those two women were woven together with

Elizabeth's and Mary's of so many generations ago. Together they rejoiced in the knowledge of the joy of life and the laughter of children. Today, Sharon is in her own Elizabeth phase of life and is attempting to impart these same truths to her young Marys.

If you are in your Mary phase, be openhearted to the Elizabeths in your life as they pass your way. Watch for them. When you least expect it, they will be there. If you are in your Elizabeth phase, remember that actions often speak louder than words. Let your heart message be constant and kind in its mentoring. There are Marys everywhere who are watching and praying for an Elizabeth such as you.

JOSEPH'S ENCOURAGING VOICE

Scripture doesn't indicate exactly how long Mary stayed with Elizabeth. Some estimate that she may have remained until the time of John's birth. That would have been approximately three months. We don't know if there was any obvious change in Mary's appearance when she went back home. However, we do have some indication this is possibly true.

Matthew 1:18 says that "she was found to be with child." Some scholars interpret this as meaning she was noticeably pregnant. They deem that the original language of this passage indicates that she looked as though she had a "ball in her stomach."

Mary's cousin Elizabeth had been so accepting and encouraging. She had told Mary about her condition before Mary could even speak it to her. But what about Joseph? What would he think of this "ball in her stomach"?

In Mary's culture, if Joseph had decided to openly expose her pregnancy, she could have been stoned to death. At the very least, he had the right to divorce her. Again, Mary had to let God do the talking. Joseph needed to hear from God himself, even though he was a righteous man who didn't want to humiliate Mary or separate himself from her.

We must allow God to speak to the significant people in our lives. It's not always easy for others to accept our decisions or accept what we feel about the children the Lord has given us. Even though others may be very close to you, they do not see your child in the way you do. They, too, need to receive an enabling grace from the Lord if they are going to be effectively and significantly involved in your child's life. In practical terms, this means that you may need to give them some emotional space to sort the issues out before the Lord.

In Matthew 1:20, when it says that Joseph "considered this," it means that he was turning the matter over in his mind. As he thought about it over and over, he fell asleep and began to dream.

The angel appeared and spoke to him. He simply told Joseph not to be afraid to take Mary as his wife. Then he gave Joseph the details of the prophetic fulfillment surrounding these events.

I love how Joseph responded. Scripture simply says, "He did what the angel of the Lord had commanded him" (Matt. 1:24). When God spoke, Joseph obeyed. He was a man of simple faith and obedience. Through that response, God would make him the most privileged stepfather ever to walk the earth.

We have no record that Joseph ever did anything short of honoring Mary. He led his family in every appropriate way possible. I wonder if he always, or if he ever, felt adequate to do the job set before him. God had given him this beautiful wife and son to love and to cherish. How would he go about it? No one had trained him how to raise the Son of God, yet this is what was being asked of him. How would he do it? He would probably do it much like you or I would—one day at a time.

I have a wonderful brother-in-law, Tim, who is much like Joseph. He, too, is partnering with his wife in raising some very beautiful children. He's doing his best to impart what he loves to his children. For Joseph it was carpentry. For this young father, at this juncture in his parenting, it's a love for the great outdoors.

One day Tim took his two-year-old son, Jesse, for his first fishing trip. The plan was to take him to a pond that was specially stocked with fish for children to easily catch. When they arrived, much to Tim's dismay, the pond was not open for business yet. So he took little Jesse to a nearby place to fish. He did this without really having much hope of catching anything.

My brother-in-law got pint-sized Jesse all set with his pole and bait and put his line in the water. He started to walk back to the car for more supplies when Jesse began to yell, "Daddy! Daddy! Fishy! Fishy!" Tim turned and could see Jesse's line bobbing in the water. He yelled for him to let go of the pole, as it was pulling him closer to the water; but Jesse continued to yell. "Daddy! Fishy! Fishy!" Tim got there in time to help the little guy pull a 17-inch fish out of the water. He had to literally pry Jesse's little fingers off the pole after they got the fish in.

The story goes on. A local game warden came by and suspiciously eyed the fish. (It was legal for children under 12 to fish without a license, but not adults.) He asked Tim if he had a license and was told no. The warden then said, "You don't expect me to believe this little guy caught that fish, do you?" Tim assured him that Jesse had indeed caught the fish. The warden indulgently told him to be careful and assured him that another game warden might not be so tolerant.

As the game warden was walking up the hill to leave, little Jesse put his line back in the water and it began to bob. He once again yelled, "Daddy! Daddy! Fishy! Fishy!" The game warden turned around to see him pull in a 16-inch. The game warden said, "If I hadn't seen it myself, I wouldn't have believed it!" Jesse caught two more fish that day!

I wonder if that's how people felt about Joseph's boy, Jesus. I wonder if his integrity was ever questioned in Nazareth because of the kind of fishing stories that went around about Jesus.

Yes, Joseph was definitely an important "other" for Mary. His integrity, spiritual intuitiveness, and humility were all keys to the success of her personal journey. His willingness to grasp the vision himself was significant. His willingness to be obedient must have meant so much to this brave young mother. Together they would go many places with this unique child.

WHO ARE YOUR "OTHERS"?

We all need help from time to time in our mothering journey. Be wise like Mary and seek out the kind of people who can give you strength.

First and foremost, remember that "the Lord is with you" (Luke 1:28).

Next, find an Elizabeth. Find someone who can identify with you in your journey. She may be old or young, but she must be true and full of faith. Find a woman who is humble, is full of integrity and will speak faith and encouragement to the very depths of your soul. When you're down, let her do her job and tell you, "Blessed are you among women, and blessed is the child you bear!" (Luke 1:42).

To those of you who are married, look for the Joseph in your husband. Honor him in his calling and vocation, and appreciate his genuine efforts to provide for you and the family. Whether he is a Christian or not, most husbands respond to wives who genuinely appreciate their efforts to make wise decisions and provide for the family.

Finally, if you are not married, discover your Joseph. Find a man who will pray for you and with you. Find a man who will listen to you and hear from God himself. Find a man who is faithful and will not leave you or degrade you in times of trouble. Look for a man who is spiritually alert and quick to obey God. When all is said and done, make sure he is a man who will "take you home as his wife" (Matt. 1:24).

Notes

1. "Trust His Heart," copyright 1988. Tourmaline Music, Inc. (BMI). Administered by SONGS FOR THE PLANET, INC., at P.O. Box 271056, Nashville, Tennessee 37227. International Copyright Secured. All Rights Reserved. Used by permission.
2. *A Mother Is to Cherish* (Nashville: Thomas Nelson Publishers, 1994), n.p.

Chapter 4

DECLARATIONS OF FAITH

When Elizabeth heard Mary's greeting, the baby leaped in her womb,
and Elizabeth was filled with the Holy Spirit. In a loud voice she exclaimed:
"Blessed are you among women, and blessed is the child you will bear!
But why am I so favored, that the mother of my Lord should come to me?
As soon as the sound of your greeting reached my ears, the baby in my womb
leaped for joy. Blessed is she who has believed that what the Lord has said
to her will be accomplished!"
And Mary said: "My soul glorifies the Lord and my spirit rejoices in God my
Savior, for he has been mindful of the humble state of his servant.
From now on all generations will call me blessed, for the Mighty One has done
great things for me—holy is his name. His mercy extends to those who fear
him, from generation to generation. He has performed mighty deeds with his
arm; he has scattered those who are proud in their inmost thoughts.
He has brought down rulers from their thrones but has lifted up the humble.
He has filled the hungry with good things but has sent the rich away empty.
He has helped his servant Israel, remembering to be merciful to Abraham and
his descendants forever, even as he said to our fathers."

LUKE 1:41-55

Elizabeth's response at the moment of Mary's arrival at her house brought immense joy to Mary's spirit and bestowed on her great honor. How amazing that Elizabeth would speak such things! After all, Elizabeth was the one who was the respected wife of a priest as well as a daughter of Aaron. Her words seemed so immediate and yet so prophetic. *Could this indeed be my confirmation of Gabriel's message?* Mary wondered.

Something began to rise up from deep within her soul. It seemed that the past, present and future were converging in harmony. Oh, such sweet melody! The depth of her soul responded to the depth of the words Elizabeth uttered. Deep called to deep. Waters of revelation seemed to rush over Mary's soul. Her cup of blessing was full and running over. She had to sing what was in her heart or surely she would burst!

Have you ever wondered what went through Mary's mind when her aged cousin, Elizabeth, proclaimed her "the mother of my Lord"? Her mind must have raced as her spirit filled with prophetic insight and joyous melody. It had been only a few seconds, but she couldn't contain it any longer.

What is this greeting Elizabeth is proclaiming within my ears? Her very words bear witness with Gabriel's message. Indeed, I must be walking under a canopy of blessing! I am blessed, my child is blessed and what has been spoken will be accomplished! My heart is overflowing!

I'm bursting with God-news; I'm dancing the song of my Savior God. God took one good look at me, and look what happened—I'm the most fortunate woman on earth! What God has done for me will never be forgotten, the God whose very name is holy, set apart from all others. His mercy flows in wave after wave on those who are in awe before him. He bared his arm and showed his strength, scattered the bluffing braggarts. He knocked tyrants off their high horses, pulled victims out of the mud. The starving poor sat down to a banquet; the callous rich were left out in the cold. He embraced his chosen child, Israel; he remembered and piled on the mercies, piled them high. It's exactly what he promised, beginning with Abraham and right up to now (Luke 1:46-55, *The Message*).

Have you ever felt so overwhelmed with the goodness of God that you could barely contain yourself? Have you ever felt so excited about the potential you saw in your child that you wanted to stand and cheer, "That's my child"? Have you ever felt so proud of your child that you almost felt sorry for every other parent in the room? Have you ever just wanted to shout, "It's me and that's mine—how about that"?

Upon reaching her destination and hearing Elizabeth's proclamation, Mary could barely contain herself. She was filled with melody that intertwined her present joy with the harmony of the ages. She could do nothing short of bursting into song as her heart overflowed with exaltation and prophetic revelation. This was indeed a stellar musical, not to be performed on stage, but where the home fires burned brightly.

Mary totally abandoned herself to the Lord and His purposes. She declared her commitment to God and declared her gratitude. Then prophetic insight flooded her soul and the resident song within her was released.

HANNAH'S SONG

There was another woman in biblical history who proclaimed a similar message. Her name was Hannah. She was the mother of the prophet Samuel. She, too, had abandoned herself and her son to God's purposes. She, too, had something to herald.

Unlike Mary, Hannah had been married for many years prior to the birth of her son. In desperation for a child, Hannah prayed, "O LORD Almighty, if you will only look upon your servant's misery and remember me, and not forget your servant but give her a son, then I will give him to the LORD for all the days of his life" (1 Sam. 1:11).

The Lord heard and answered Hannah's prayer. He blessed her with a son. After she weaned him, she brought him to the Temple of the Lord as she had promised. In bringing him to the priest, she said, "I prayed for this child, and the LORD has granted me what I asked of him. So now I give him to the LORD. For his whole life he will be given over to the LORD" (1 Sam. 1:27,28).

Upon making this dedication, her heart rejoiced and prophetic insight flooded her soul. In that instant, her soul became intertwined not only with the young Mary of the future but with her Messiah as well.

Hannah's acclamation met with Mary's song across the ages as she proclaimed:

> *My heart exults in the LORD; my strength is exalted in the LORD. My mouth derides my enemies, because I rejoice in thy salvation. There is none holy like the LORD, there is none besides thee; there is no rock like our God. Talk no more so very proudly, let not arrogance come from your mouth; for the LORD is a God of knowledge, and by him actions are weighed. The bows of the mighty are broken, but the feeble gird on strength. Those who were full have hired themselves out for bread, but those who were hungry have ceased to hunger. The barren has borne seven, but she who has many children is forlorn. The LORD kills and brings to life; he brings down to Sheol and raises up. The LORD makes poor and makes rich; he brings low, he also exalts. He raises up the poor from the dust; he lifts the needy from the ash heap, to*

make them sit with princes and inherit a seat of honor. For the pillars of the earth are the LORD's, and on them he has set the world. He will guard the feet of his faithful ones; but the wicked shall be cut off in darkness; for not by might shall a man prevail. The adversaries of the LORD shall be broken to pieces; against them he will thunder in heaven. The LORD will judge the ends of the earth; he will give strength to his king, and exalt the power of his anointed (1 Sam. 2:1-10, *RSV*).

Through their heart responses to God, Mary's and Hannah's affirmations were interlaced as a harmonious duet throughout the ages. Through these two mothers, God networked the old with the new.

Both women had a prayer of gratefulness and prophetic proclamation. Both were enraptured with God's goodness to them and to the generations to come. From both came a resounding, "My spirit has rejoiced in God!"

At this point, both mothers still faced their greatest challenges. Mary still had to face Joseph, Simeon, Anna and the multitude of people who would send her son to the Cross. Hannah still had to wean her son and give him up to an undiscerning priest who had raised reprobate sons. She also had to face the surprise and confusion of her husband, Elkanah, as well as the continued mockery of Peninnah.

Yes, challenges were still in the forecast, but these two women chose to relish the moment and rejoice in it. This pattern of gratefulness would carry them through the events yet to come.

How long has it been since you have rejoiced in God's goodness? How long since an expression of joy and delight in the Lord has found a way into your heart and out of your mouth?

It is in focused faith in God's good will for you and your child that you will discover His blessings.

If you are in a season when children are crawling out of their beds and waking you up before your body has adequately rested, that's all the more reason to take a moment to focus. I'm not suggesting an hour of prayer on your knees, just a simple "Good morning, Lord—I'm choosing to rejoice in Your presence today."

If it has been awhile since you've started your day off with focused gratefulness to the Lord, I encourage you to take a minute and do it. Don't focus on the impossibles; focus on the possibles. If your child is in a difficult season, focus not on his or her weakness but rather on the power of God's grace working in that child.

Whether you approach your day with joy and faith or with sorrow and apprehension will be determined by your early-morning focus. That, in and of itself, can influence your child's attitude and perspective on his or her potential.

Whether you can see the blessings of God in your child or not, they are there. Hebrews 11:1,2 says, "Now faith is being sure of what we hope for and certain of what we do not see. This is what the ancients were commended for." It is in focused faith in God's good will for you and your child that you will discover His blessings.

FOCUSED ON GOD'S GOODNESS

One brave mother I know learned early in her journey how to focus her faith. Her name is Vickie. She was 19, and her husband, Rod, was 21 when their son Jimmy was born. By medical standards, as well as their own, little Jimmy was perfect in every way. Life was going great for them, and proclamations of faith came easily.

As is typical with many new babies, Jimmy woke up a lot during the night. Although it was tiring for his parents, they didn't mind getting up with him. He was their delight.

When Jimmy was five months and twelve days old, Rod and Vickie awakened in the morning and realized they had slept through the night. Rod went to check on Jimmy and discovered he had died in the night. Vickie called the paramedics as Rod attempted to resuscitate their infant son. But there was nothing anyone could do; Jimmy was gone.

Vickie's heart cry was, "Why him? And why me?" The joy of motherhood had been ripped from her grasp. Proclamations of faith evaded her thoughts as well as her speech.

Two years later, a second son, Andy, was born. He too was vibrant and healthy. When he was five months and twelve days old, Vickie and Rod slept fitfully by his bedside, watching over every breath he took. After they passed this hurdle, they began to relax and focus their faith on life once again. Gratefulness and faith began to emerge once more.

Fifteen months later, a third son came into their lives. His name is Aaron. The morning after Aaron's birth, the doctor came in to see Vickie and told her that Aaron was born with Down's syndrome. Rod arrived at the hospital soon after the doctor's visit, and together they asked the Lord, "Why did You *bless* us with this child?" Gratefulness for this new life reigned in their spirits. There was no downcast "Why us?" in their hearts. They received little Aaron's life with joy and as a blessing from the Lord.

Rod and Vickie have made it a pattern in their lives to support and encourage all of their children. They have done their best to instill in their boys Christian principles of kindness and consideration toward others. Aaron was no exception to their tutelage in this area.

When he was eight years old, he began to compete in athletic events in the Special Olympics for handicapped children. In the fall he played volleyball, in the winter he played basketball, and in the spring he did track events.

When Aaron was 10 years old, he ran in a track event in the Special Olympics state competition. It was his first opportunity to "run for the gold." He was running the 200-meter race and was far ahead of the other children. When he was approximately 15 feet from the finish line, he stopped and waved for the other five children to hurry and run fast. One girl tripped and fell; he went back and helped her up. After all the other participants crossed over the finish line, he crossed over, shouting with joy, "I won! I won!"

This win would have been his first medal. Instead, he received a sixth-place ribbon from the judges. But he received a gold medal of pride and joy from his parents. He did indeed win. Vickie's maternal buttons were popping that day. Her heart rejoiced in the stamp of God's character on her son's life.

Today, Aaron is a young adult. By the time he was 18 years old, he had won approximately 20 bronze, silver and gold medals. Even though he learned how to win a race, he has always been known as a kind and considerate young man who brings joy to many hearts.

You can't be around Rod and Vickie for long without their joy and their grateful spirits rubbing off on you. They, like Mary and Hannah, have experienced moments of questioning, yet have found themselves standing in wonder at the goodness of God.

Not only has God blessed them now with four vibrant children who are a strong testimony for Christ, but they also have another child who is waiting for them in heaven. Truly they are forever grateful for God's good work in their lives. Truly this mother's heart proclaims along with Mary and Hannah, "My spirit has rejoiced in God!"

FAITH ANNOUNCEMENTS

There are three proclamations that both Mary and Hannah declared following their words of gratitude. They heralded the news that God had turned the tables and righted the wrongs. In doing so, they proclaimed that He was bringing death to man's pride, prejudice and greed. They proclaimed that His work in their lives was evidence of these realities, now and in the future. Everything within them shouted, "Look at me; I am evidence of God's great love! I'm just a humble woman, but God is using me and my child!"

Through these proclamations, Mary and Hannah proclaimed God's message of unfathomable love to all humanity. Their pronouncements preceded the coming of the Messiah and made an indelible mark on the generations to come, for He did come and validate their claims.

For God so loved the world that he gave his one and only Son, that whoever believes in him shall not perish but have eternal life. For God did not send his Son into the world to condemn the world, but to save the world through him. Whoever believes in him is not condemned, but whoever does not believe stands condemned already because he has not believed in the name of God's one and only Son. This is the verdict: Light has come into the world, but men loved darkness instead of light because their deeds were evil. Everyone who does evil hates the light, and will not come into the light for fear that his deeds will be exposed. But whoever lives by the truth comes into the light, so that it may be seen plainly that what he has done has been done through God (John 3:16-21).

When Jesus' human birth came through a humble maiden, He literally scattered the proud in the imagination of their hearts. He also exalted the lowly and filled the hungry.

Obviously, our children are not the coming Messiah. However, the question must be asked of every mother, What faith proclamations have you been making to your children? Perhaps your children will also have an integral part in bringing death to pride, prejudice and greed. As Christian mothers, we certainly should be modeling and teaching them to do so. What vision do you have for your children, and what are the words your children hear you speak about them?

When I was expecting my firstborn child, I read that the Muslims credited much of their success to the powerful influence of their mothers. I read that it was not uncommon for mothers to say to their children daily, "Jehovah is our God. Mohammed is our prophet."

When I read this I decided to turn it around and use it for the Lord. So when my children were babes in my arms, I continually told them, "Jesus, who is the King of kings and Lord of lords, loves you and has a special plan for your life." I repeated this as part of my nightly routine with them when they were growing up. As they got older, I changed the words a bit, but the message was the same.

These were not mere words I spoke out of reaction to another religion. These were words of life I would stake my life on. These words became so familiar that if I ever neglected to say them before I turned out the light at bedtime, my children would remind me before I left the room: "Say it, Mommy, 'Jesus loves me and has a special plan for my life.' " I would agree and then we would repeat it. The impact of those words had made their mark, and I was thankful.

Recently, I received a note from my young adult daughter, who is excited about life and the future the Lord has for her. She said, "You wrote Scriptures on my heart, and a sense of destiny and purpose. When you said every night 'Jesus has a special plan for your life,' I believed you . . . and I still do."

Just as the bedtime words were etched on the canvas of my daughter's heart, her words of appreciation and acceptance of them have indelibly marked mine. In some inalterable way, my heart rejoices and is interlaced with Mary's and Hannah's forever.

A mother's words are powerful. We must be ever faithful to speak words of reality and faith into the hearts of our children. Proverbs 18:21 says, "The tongue has the power of life and death, and those who love it will eat its fruit." Proverbs 15:4 says, "The tongue that brings healing is a tree of life."

You cannot speak into your child a destiny the Lord has not determined for him or her. However, you can instill faith and belief in them to become all that God has destined them to be. One unknown poet put it this way:

I took a piece of plastic clay
And idly fashioned it one day.
And as my fingers pressed it still,
It bent and yielded to my will
I came again when days were past,
The bit of clay was hard at last.
My early impress still it bore,
And I could change its form no more.
You take a piece of living clay
And gently form it day by day,
Molding with your power and art,
A young boy's soft and yielding heart.
You come again when years are gone,
It is a man you look upon.
Your early impress still he bore
And you can change him never more.

With all the challenges that come, motherhood is still one of the greatest blessings that will ever cross a woman's pathway. Allow me to paraphrase Matthew 5:3-11 to put these blessings into perspective.

A MOTHER'S BEATITUDES

- *Blessed is the mother* whose children freely laugh, play and pray, for hers is the kingdom of heaven on earth.
- *Blessed is the mother* who cries when she needs to but does not lack faith, for she will be comforted.
- *Blessed is the mother* who has a gentle disposition in the

midst of the fluctuating emotions of her children, for she will inherit their hearts.

- *Blessed is the mother* who hungers for a closer walk with God, for she will be nourished and sustained.
- *Blessed is the mother* who is merciful in moments of contradiction, for she will receive mercy in the days that lie ahead.
- *Blessed is the mother* who is pure in heart and in spirit, for she will see God and the future in the eyes of her children.
- *Blessed is the mother* who is a peacemaker in times of storm, for she will be called trustworthy and true.
- *Blessed is the mother* who is disheartened in the journey, for there is hope and a future for her.
- *Blessed is the mother* who alone can see her child's potential, for God Himself will be her rear guard.

Blessed mother, rejoice and be glad, because great is your reward in heaven.

Motherhood will require more than you have to give, but the blessings will far outweigh the challenges because the grace of the Lord Jesus will be with you (see 1 Cor. 16:23).

Acknowledge along with Elizabeth that you are "blessed . . . among women." Proclaim with Mary that your "soul glorifies the Lord" and your "spirit rejoices in God." In these proclamations you will find a song in your heart and a grace that will sustain you for the journey ahead.

Chapter 5

UNSPOKEN TREASURES

In those days Caesar Augustus issued a decree that a census should be taken of the

entire Roman world. . . . And everyone went to his own town to register.

So Joseph also went up from the town of Nazareth in Galilee to Judea, to

Bethlehem the town of David, because he belonged to the house and line of

David. He went there to register with Mary, who was pledged to be married to

him and was expecting a child. While they were there, the time came for the

baby to be born, and she gave birth to her firstborn, a son. . . .

And there were shepherds living out in the fields nearby, keeping watch over

their flocks at night. An angel of the Lord appeared to them, and the glory

of the Lord shone around them, and they were terrified. But the angel said to

them, "Do not be afraid. I bring you good news of great joy that will be for

all the people. Today in the town of David a Savior has been born to you;

he is Christ the Lord. This will be a sign to you: You will find a baby

wrapped in cloths and lying in a manger."

So they hurried off and found Mary and Joseph, and the baby, who was lying

in the manger. When they had seen him, they spread the word concerning what

had been told them about this child, and all who heard it were amazed at what

the shepherds said to them. But Mary treasured up all these things and

pondered them in her heart.

LUKE 2:1-12,16-19

It was nearly time for the census to be taken, yet what of Mary's condition? Her time was near. From Nazareth to Bethlehem it was almost 80 miles. That was at least a four-day journey. Would she make it?

Of late, the whispers and wonderings of the neighborhood women seemed to have ceased and Mary was confident they would be there to help at the birthing. Nazareth was home; it was a safe place for her child to be born. But what would come of her and her child in Bethlehem? Would there be a safe place for them in this bustling town?

She knew her baby was destined to be a boy, and boys were always received with such rejoicing and celebration. She and Joseph had so looked forward to hearing the song of the minstrels at the birth. But who would give her son an appropriate welcome in Bethlehem? Who would sing a song of jubilation? Any town during census time would be overcrowded with disgruntled people.

There was no getting around the fact that she and Joseph were both of the house of David, and Bethlehem was the headquarters of their tribe. They had to register and pay their poll tax or be under the judgment of Rome. So to Bethlehem they must go.

She would trust the Lord and recount the words the angel Gabriel and her cousin Elizabeth had spoken to her so many months ago. She must fasten her hopes on this resolve: Her child would indeed be born.

I wonder if her thoughts during this time went something like this:

Oh, Lord, a four-day journey! I don't know if I can make it! The trip to Elizabeth's and back, even though longer, was nothing in comparison to this. I was so, well . . . so unencumbered in my body then. Lord, are You sure You and the Roman Empire have your timetables coordinated?

Yes, Lord, I am Your servant. Yes, I know I said, "May it be to me as You have said." If this is part of it, I'm with You. I have to admit that I have been reminded recently of Micah's passage: "But, you Bethlehem . . . out of you will come for me one who will be ruler over Israel, whose origins are from of old, from ancient times" (Mic. 5:2). Could it be? Oh, Lord, my mind can go in so many directions at once!

Back to this trip. Lord, I have just two little requests. Would You please provide a private place for Joseph and me that we might drink in the wonder of Your gift to us? Also, wherever this child is born, would You please send some minstrels with a song of jubilation? I'd like the song to match the praise I have in my heart for You and Your wondrous works.

Thank You, Father. You're my best friend. I do trust You. As King Solomon wrote so long ago, I know that You have "made everything beautiful in its time" (Eccles. 3:11). To walk with You is to be in peace, so off to Bethlehem we go. Truly, "Your word is a lamp to my feet and a light for my path" (Ps. 119:105).

Have you ever been confused about the events in your life and then suddenly realized the hand of God was at work? Have you ever been so amazed at your thoughts concerning your child that you dare not do anything more than ponder them in your heart? Have you ever thought that if people really knew what you could see in your child, they would dismiss you as a foolish, nearsighted woman? Have you ever marveled so at the goodness of God that you were left speechless?

That is what it must have been like for Mary. God was so ordering her steps that every detail was seemingly outlined to the minutest detail.

Have you ever been so amazed at your thoughts concerning your child that you dare not do anything more than ponder them in your heart?

Although ancient census records show that people had to return to their hometowns for a tax census, the city to which they returned was where they owned property, not simply where they were born. Not only had Joseph been born and probably raised in Bethlehem, but he also possibly owned property there. This would have been considered his legal residence, even though he lived in Nazareth. One copy of an actual government edict from Egypt said:

Gaius Vibius Maximus, Prefect of Egypt, orders: "Seeing that the time has come for the house-to-house census, it is necessary to compel all those who for any cause whatsoever are residing outside their districts to return to their own homes, that they may both carry out the regular order of the census, and may also diligently attend to the cultivation of their allotments."[1]

Although the tax laws in most of the Roman Empire required only the head of a household to appear, women over the age of 12 were also taxed. Mary would not have been required to appear to register, but Joseph must not have wanted to leave her behind with the birth so near.

When you consider the increased traffic a census would have brought into little Bethlehem, it would be easy to imagine that people were murmuring about Rome's oppression, as well as the burden of taxation and inconvenience of travel. All of this murmuring and complaining would have been going on while a Savior was being born in their midst. Often while we're complaining, God is at work.

Inns with no vacancy would be prophetically symbolic of what was to happen to Jesus. One day in the future, the only place for Him would be on a cross.

How often do we, as mothers, get so consumed and overcrowded in our schedules that we miss the birth of Christ in our daily lives? How often do we relegate Him to a lonely cross?

Hundreds of years prior to this time, Micah proclaimed, "But, you Bethlehem . . . out of you will come for me one who will be ruler over Israel, whose origins are from of old, from ancient times" (Mic. 5:2). For Jesus to be born in busy little Bethlehem would fulfill this prophecy and establish His covenant connection with David.

So the steps of Joseph and Mary were ordered to bring about this fulfillment. Why Mary? Why Bethlehem? Why now? Because God had so ordered it.

GOD'S TIMETABLE

How many mothers do you know whose children came at the "wrong" time? According to your plans, were you one of those mothers?

That would have been the testimony of a friend of mine a few years ago. She is a single mother of two beautiful children. One of her children seemed to have arrived at the perfect time; the other arrived at a time that would have baffled most.

My friend was married to a wonderful, sensitive, talented man who was full of life and had a gift to teach. Their marriage had some of the typical problems that most young marriages have, but they were happy. The main point of frustration for her was her inability to conceive. She desperately wanted to experience the joy of motherhood.

After making the decision to place herself under medical supervision, she began to take fertility drugs. Much to her delight one day, the news came that they were to have a child. Her husband came home with two dozen roses in hand. Several months later they were blessed with the life of their first child. God had indeed worked a miracle.

Although their first child was a constant joy to them, my friend began to earnestly desire to have another child. Much to her dismay, the months and years continued to turn over as easily as the pages on a calendar.

Unknown to her, her husband had begun to struggle in other areas in his life. It seemed that the sunshine of their home was overcome by an encompassing fog of despair. She tried to hold fast to the dreams within their grasp, but her husband's hand began to slip from hers. Sadness entered where there had once been joy; frustration replaced love; confusion conquered the peace that was once theirs.

It was the fall season when he left. How appropriate it seemed. Leaves were falling and so was their hope. The sparkle of love and dreams that once filled their hearts seemed illusive and unreachable. They tried to reach each other, but the love that once burned brightly was obscured by many hurtful choices.

Were there no more miracles to be discovered? Were there no more hidden riches yet to be revealed? Was there a miracle to be found in the approaching Christmas season?

Her monthly cycle had been so irregular with all of the recent stress that she hadn't given its absence much thought. But then there was this feeling inside of her. Could it be? Surely not. She decided to restore her peace of mind by purchasing a pregnancy test.

Much to her surprise and delight, new life was once again within her womb. Initially, she was thrilled with the miracle inside of her. But to her sorrow, her now ex-husband's response was "Why now?"

After the birth of her child, as she realized how complicated her life had become, she too wondered about the Lord's timing. What was this miracle that lay resting in her arms? Why now, in the midst of a broken marriage covenant?

The answer to her ponderings would be the same as Mary's: Because God had so ordered it. She, like Mary, would see that "No eye has seen, no ear has heard, no mind has conceived what God has prepared for those who love Him" (1 Cor. 2:9; cf., Isa. 64:4).

She would find this great Shepherd to be faithful where there had been unfaithfulness, understanding where there had been misunderstanding, and caring where there had been neglect. She would not be removed from her reality, but she would be swept into His all-encompassing grace, time and time again.

Did she wonder about the timing and possible destiny of this child? Yes, she did. Were her meditations many? Yes, they were. But along with Mary, it was in this specific truth—that God had so ordered it—that her hope found a place to abide.

Do you ever wonder about the timing and possible destiny of your child? Are your meditations many? Listen closely and see if you can hear the meditations of your child's heart. Does your child sing to the Lord with David of old?

> Oh yes, you shaped me first inside, then out; you formed me in my mother's womb. I thank you, High God— you're breathtaking! Body and soul, I am marvelously made! I worship in adoration—what a creation! You know me inside and out, you know every bone in my body; You know exactly how I was made, bit by bit, how I was sculpted from nothing into something. Like an open book, you watched me grow from conception to birth; all the stages of my life were spread out before you, the days of my life all prepared before I'd even lived one day. Your thoughts—how rare, how beautiful! God, I'll never comprehend them! I couldn't even begin to count them—any more than I could count the sand of the sea. Oh, let me rise in the morning and live always with you! (Ps. 139:13-18, *The Message*).

What a song, what a proclamation! Why me, you ask? Why this child, and why now? Because God has so ordered it. You are His "highly favored one" for this specific child at this specific time. His promise to you is, as it was to Mary so many years ago, "No eye has seen, no ear has heard, no mind has conceived what God has prepared for those who love him" (1 Cor. 2:9). It is in this truth that your hope can find a place to abide.

UNLIKELY RECEIVERS OF GOD'S NEWS

Shepherding was not considered an honorable trade in the Jewish culture. It was a very demanding trade. Because of this the shepherds were unable to keep the details of the Jewish ceremonial law. All of the meticulous hand-washing rules and regulations were beyond the demands of their daily lifestyle. Even participation in the normal religious activities of their communities was uncommon for them.

Because they were nomadic, they were also assumed to be the thieves when local sheep were missing. They were commonly categorized as sinners among their own people. I wonder if God sent the angels to the shepherds first as an indication of the sinners to whom He was sending His Son.

It is possible that the shepherds the angels visited were the shepherds who watched over the flocks destined for Temple sacrifices at Passover. Just think! Those tending the Passover lambs would be among the first to see the Lamb of God, who would be sacrificed for the sins of the world.

It was to these humble sinners that the song of jubilation and revelation would come and the Lamb of God would be revealed.

If Mary had been disappointed that there were no earthly minstrels to sing with jubilation when her son was born, she would be blessed to hear the reports that angels had sung the song no earthly singer could. This song of praise was beyond anything she could have imagined.

The Archko Volume chronicles a written interview of the shepherds by a young man named Jonathan who was a servant to a Jewish priest in Bethlehem at the time. Here is a portion of his report to the Sanhedrin:

> When they were aroused, it was light as day. But they knew it was not daylight, for it was only the third watch. All at once the air seemed to be filled with human voices, saying, "Glory! Glory! Glory to the most high God!" and "Happy are thou, Bethlehem, for God hath fulfilled His

promise to the fathers; for in thy chambers is born the King that shall rule in righteousness." Their shoutings would rise up in the heavens and then would sink down in mellow strains and roll along at the foot of the mountains, and die away in the most soft and musical manner they had ever heard; then it would begin again high up in the heavens, in the very vaults of the sky, and descend in sweet and melodious strains, so that they could not refrain from shouting and weeping at the same time. The light would seem to burst forth high up in the heavens, and then descend in softer rays, and light up the hills and valleys, making everything more visible than the light of the sun, though it was not so brilliant, but clearer, like the brightest moon. (The interviewer continues.) I asked them how they felt—if they were not afraid; they said at first they were; but after a while it seemed to calm their spirits, and so fill their hearts with love and tranquility that they felt more like giving thanks than anything else.[2]

This specific account is not in the Bible. So whether the details are accurate or not, we do not know. However, from the biblical account in Luke, we do know that what the shepherds reported to Mary (and Joseph) caused her to quietly ponder their words in her heart. We also know the shepherds spread the word throughout Bethlehem and "all who heard it were amazed at what the shepherds said to them" (Luke 2:18). We also know they "returned, glorifying and praising God for all the things they had heard and seen, which were just as they had been told" (Luke 2:20).

AN UNLIKELY RECEIVER OF GOD'S VISION
There was another mother in contemporary Church history who had things to ponder about one of her children. Her name was

Sarah Mumford. Having lost three infant sons to death by the time her only daughter, Catherine, was born, she considered her to be a special gift.

Catherine was a very active and observant child who had a keen imagination. Without being formally taught, she quickly learned her letters and could read by the age of three. She so loved the exciting stories of the Bible that by the time she was twelve years old she had read it through eight times.

One day Catherine was so intrigued by the story of young Samuel hearing God's call that she asked her mother, "Did the Lord ever speak in such a way to a little girl like me?" Her mother smiled and began to tell her the story in 2 Kings 5:1-14. She said, "That part of history tells us that Naaman, the head of the Syrian army, suffered from the dreadful disease of leprosy. Naaman's wife had a Jewish slave girl. This little maid was impressed by the Lord to tell her mistress that her husband could be healed if he would go to the prophet Elisha and follow his instructions."

She continued the story of how Naaman obeyed the prophet and washed seven times in the Jordan River. She said, "When he came out of the water, the Bible says that his 'flesh came again like the flesh of a little child, and he was clean.' "

At that point young Catherine looked at her own clear skin and asked, "Could God work through another little girl in our time?"

"Of course," replied her mother.

"Even a little girl like me?"

"Yes, even a little girl like you."

Another time, while doing one of her daily chores of carrying in a fresh supply of wood for the household fire, Catherine asked, "Mama, will the Lord answer my prayers?"

"Of course. Why do you ask?" her mother responded.

"Because there are so many things in this world that are

wrong. There are children who have to go to bed without having anything to eat all day. Think, Mama, how simply dreadful it must be to go to bed hungry!" Wiping away tears, she continued, "I almost wish I could give my portion of the cake to a poor family I know."

Today we know that this young, tenderhearted girl went on to become the cofounder of the Salvation Army, alongside her husband, William Booth. Her husband often asked her to help him with his sermons, as he was known to say, "You know the Bible better than I do." As a speaker, she filled some of the largest auditoriums in England. She wrote books and became the "mother" of this "army" that still feeds and clothes the poor today.[3]

I wonder if her mother pondered Catherine's thought-provoking questions long after their discussions ended. I wonder if she ever dreamed that her daughter would write, speak to thousands and be responsible for sharing the love of Christ with so many poor in such practical ways. I wonder if she ever imagined that the influence of her daughter's life would cross the ocean to another continent.

HOLDING ON TO GOD'S HAND

I have a friend who recently became a grandmother for the first time. Her name is Randi. Interestingly enough, she is one of the great-granddaughters of William and Catherine Booth, by an extended-family relationship. She, like Catherine's mother, Sarah Mumford, has much to ponder about her children.

Recently, when she shared current photos and the delights of her new role as a grandmother, she concluded our conversation by saying, "My cup of blessing is full." With a look of wonder and a tear in her eye she repeated, "My cup of blessing is full." Not only had she meditated on the wonder of God in the lives of her children when they were young, but also now she was pondering the goodness of God in their adult years.

She has three young adult children. The oldest is married and is the one who presented her with the title of grandmother. The second was voted by his classmates to be the student body president of his college. The third has finished her second year in college and is being nothing short of a blessing to her mother as well. To top it off, all of her children are actively serving the Lord. Indeed, her "cup of blessing is full."

When she made this statement, I was reminded of a story I heard her second son, Jason, tell in a college chapel service. He said that when he was just a little guy he loved to walk to the store with his mother and hold her hand.

As they walked along, Jason would slip his hand out of his mother's and say, "You're not holding on tight enough, Mommy." She would smile and once again take hold of his hand. He would wait awhile and then slip his hand out of her trusting grasp and scold, "You're not holding on tight enough." She would chuckle and say, "Okay," and take his hand once again. When his hand was unable to find its momentary release, he would adoringly commend her, "That's good, Mommy."

This was part of their familiar journey to the store and back. It was a playful ritual of enduring trust and loving assurance of a mother's care for her son. Through the years she held tightly to her God and taught her children how to do so as well.

Jason has now become a mentor to other children, teaching them how to hold tightly to the hand of God. Like Catherine Booth, he too has a desire to reach out to those in need. He now holds the hands of those in need by reaching out to children raised in inner-city neighborhoods. I wonder what he ponders as he takes hold of their trusting hands. I wonder if they too slip their hands away as an inquisitive test. The lesson of trust engraved on his own heart is one he now etches on the hearts of others.

Jason's mother, Randi, had simple, yet profound, thoughts concerning all of her children. She faithfully brought those ponderings before the Lord in prayer many times over the years. In doing so, she transformed her meditations into fruitfulness through the lives of her children and grandchildren.

How precious, how sweet are the ponderings of mothers, both young and old. How faithful and how prolific, as a mother's meditations become intercessions, and intercessions become fruit that feeds a generation—all for the Master's use.

You may not have shepherds coming to tell you of angelic proclamations concerning your children, but join in the chorus and herald the good news: "Glory to God in the highest, and on earth peace to men [and women] on whom His favor rests" (Luke 2:14).

His favor rests with you. Treasure up all these things and ponder them in your heart, for these unspoken treasures are your hidden riches both now and in the years to come. Cherish them as you would a family heirloom. If you do, you may find that your spirit will sing in chorus with Randi's, "My cup of blessing is full."

Notes

1. William Barclay, *The Daily Study Bible, The Gospel of Luke* (Edinburgh: The Saint Andrew Press, 1975), p. 21.
2. Drs. McIntosh and Twyman, *The Archko Volume or the Archeological Writings of the Sanhedrim and Talmuds of the Jews* (New Canaan, Conn.: Keats Publishing, 1975), p. 65.
3. Charles Ludwig, *Mother of an Army* (Minneapolis: Bethany House Publishers, 1987), p. 15.

Section Three

THE EARLY YEARS
OF PREPARATION

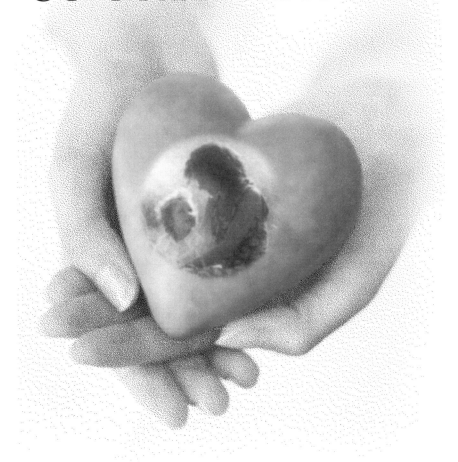

Chapter 6

RELEASING THROUGH CONSECRATION

*When the time of their purification according to the Law of Moses had been
completed, Joseph and Mary took him to Jerusalem to present him to the Lord
(as it is written in the Law of the Lord, "Every firstborn male is to be consecrated
to the Lord"), and to offer a sacrifice in keeping with what is said in the Law
of the Lord: "a pair of doves or two young pigeons."
Now there was a man in Jerusalem called Simeon, who was righteous and
devout. He was waiting for the consolation of Israel, and the Holy Spirit was
upon him. It had been revealed to him by the Holy Spirit that he would not die
before he had seen the Lord's Christ. Moved by the Spirit, he went into the temple
courts. When the parents brought in the child Jesus to do for him what the custom
of the Law required, Simeon took him in his arms and praised God, saying:
"Sovereign Lord, as you have promised, you now dismiss your servant in peace.
For my eyes have seen your salvation, which you have prepared in the sight of all
people, a light for revelation to the Gentiles and for glory to your people Israel."
The child's father and mother marveled at what was said about him.
Then Simeon blessed them and said to Mary, his mother: "This child is destined
to cause the falling and rising of many in Israel, and to be a sign that will be
spoken against, so that the thoughts of many hearts will be revealed.
And a sword will pierce your own soul too."*

LUKE 2:22-35

Thirty-two days had passed since Mary and Joseph had taken the baby to the local synagogue to be circumcised and receive his name. They did this in obedience to what God had told Abram long ago, "For the generations to come every male among you who is eight days old must be circumcised" (Gen. 17:12). This message had been engraved in their hearts since childhood, and they responded appropriately on this important day of their son's life.

Although, according to their custom, Mary was still considered ceremonially impure at the time of this important event, she rejoiced from a distance during the sacred ceremony. This was the day that signified her son's covenant with God as an individual on His own. He had been in her arms a mere eight days and now she had released Him to begin His new cycle of life, not from within her, but from without.

Her day of purification had finally arrived. It was amazing how long 40 days could seem. Not only was this her day of purification, but it was a special day for baby Jesus as well. Today he would experience the ceremony of The Redemption of the Firstborn. How exciting it was to fulfill the word the Lord had spoken to Moses so long ago: "Consecrate to me every firstborn male. The first offspring of every womb among the Israelites belongs to me" (Exod. 13:2).

There was so much to accomplish in one day! But Jerusalem was only six miles from Bethlehem and Mary was sure the journey would pass quickly. She and Joseph had their two pigeons and their babe in arms, and it was the right time; so off they went. The wonder of the ensuing ceremony filled her mind.

Oh, God, my heart is so full on this day. What wonders You have performed! Thank You that I can go to the Temple today. Thank You that I can publicly present my child to You. Every day I present Him to You, but this day is special, Lord. It's Your day; it's my day; it's His day—it's ours. Thank You, Father, for Your Redemption!

I do wish Joseph could walk a little faster, and yet I know he keeps the pace steady for my sake. What a kind and gentle husband You have given me. Though we are not rich in worldly goods, we are rich in Your goodness. I am so anxious to meet with You in the Temple. Truly, my heart goes faster than my steps.

Prepare my heart, Lord, to hear Your voice. Tell me more, Father, about this child. Guide me in the way I should go. Do not let Your glory depart from me.

The psalmist's words ring in my spirit, "I will also appoint him my firstborn, the most exalted of the kings of the earth. I will maintain my love to him forever, and my covenant with him will never fail. I will establish his line forever, his throne as long as the heavens endure" (Ps. 89:27-29).

Once again I proclaim that surely "your word is a lamp to my feet and a light for my path" (Ps. 119:105). *Guide me, Lord, and establish my steps. Make my heart ready to receive Your word.*

Can you identify with Mary? Have you ever looked at your child and wondered what the Lord had in mind when He created this little one and placed him or her in your arms? Have you ever wondered what really took place from God's perspective when you offered your child back in dedication to Him? Have you ever wondered what you and the Lord would do together with that offering?

In Mary's day it was the Jewish custom for a woman who had given birth to be considered ceremonially impure for a season of time. She could go about her household chores and daily business, but she could not participate in any religious ceremonies nor could she enter the Temple. If she had given birth to a baby boy, this period was for 40 days. If it was a girl, it was for 80 days.

At the end of this time she had to bring to the Temple a lamb offering (or two doves or pigeons if she was poor). This was offered up as a sin offering unto the Lord. At this same time she was allowed to present the child to the priest to be publicly presented to the Lord.

This presentation was not a redemptive act that cleansed the child from sin; rather, it was a consecration of the child to the Lord. It was an act of setting the child aside for a special purpose, deeming the child as holy to the Lord.

In Protestant religions today, new mothers are not considered to be impure after the birth of a child. However, they usually bring their new little one to the house of the Lord to present the baby, not only to their friends but also to the Lord. Many churches have a ceremony in which they dedicate the child to the Lord, symbolic of consecrating the child to the Lord's purposes.

A baby's ceremonial dedication is not considered as a sacrament of the Church. However, it is more than a mere extension of Judaism; it is also evidenced in Scripture throughout the ministry of Jesus. Mothers often brought their children to Him to receive His rabbinical blessing as He traveled from place to place, preaching the good news of the kingdom of God. Surely this is a pattern for us today, just as the rest of His earthly walk was.

After observing baby dedication ceremonies many times through the years, I have made a few observations. Babies who are placed into a pastor's unfamiliar arms and positioned closely to his booming voice are often startled by the adult world around them. They may look like they're praising the Lord as they raise their arms and shout, but they're really not.

Actually, this whole process, though sacred, is risky for all involved. If the baby is handed over to the minister in a familiar feeding position and this person is ill equipped to meet that need, you're bound to have a screaming child for the duration of the dedicatory prayer.

When you hand your child to the minister, try not to hand him a wet or hungry baby. For that matter, if you've recently fed the baby, make sure he or she has been properly burped or else your child and your minister will be on the brink of momentary disaster rather than holy bonding!

When Mary, Joseph and baby Jesus arrived in Jerusalem, they met a man named Simeon, even before they got inside the Temple. The Lord had promised Simeon that he would not die until he had seen the Lord's Christ. This day, Simeon had been led by the Holy Spirit to go to the Temple.

Simeon was known as one of "the quiet of the land." These were people who were known for waiting quietly and patiently on God for the revelation of the Messiah. They believed in a life of constant prayer and quiet watchfulness until He would come. Simeon was in tune with the prophetic revelation of the coming of the Messiah as outlined in the last four verses of Daniel 9.

Seventy "sevens" are decreed for your people and your holy city to finish transgression, to put an end to sin, to atone for wickedness, to bring in everlasting righteousness, to seal up vision and prophecy and to anoint the most holy. Know and understand this: From the issuing of the decree to restore and rebuild Jerusalem until the Anointed One, the ruler, comes, there will be seven "sevens," and sixty-two "sevens." It will be rebuilt with streets and a trench, but in times of trouble. After the sixty-two "sevens," the Anointed One will be cut off and will have nothing. The people of the ruler who will come will destroy the city and the sanctuary. The end will come like a flood: War will continue until the end, and desolations have been decreed. He will confirm a covenant with many for one "seven." In the middle of the "seven" he will put an end to sacrifice and offering. And on a wing of the temple he will set up an abomination that causes desolation, until the end that is decreed is poured out on him.

Simeon's spirit must have been filled with this passage of Scripture as he prophesied, "For my eyes have seen your salvation, which you have prepared in the sight of all people, a light for revelation to the Gentiles and for glory to your people Israel" (Luke 2:30-32). Little did he know that the first sermon Jesus would preach some 30 years later would be, "The time has come . . ." (Mark 1:15), as a fulfillment of Daniel 9:24-27.

Simeon blessed Mary and Joseph and the babe, and then spoke directly to Mary: "This child is destined to cause the falling and rising of many in Israel, and to be a sign that will be spoken against, so that the thoughts of many hearts will be revealed. And *a sword will pierce your own soul too*" (Luke 2:34,35, italics added).

Just as Simeon finished speaking, an aged woman, who was a prophetess named Anna, came up to them. When she saw the babe, she began to praise God and preach about the child to all those around who also had been watching and waiting.

What a party it must have been!—although I do wonder if while the praise party was going on, Mary was contemplating Simeon's words. I wonder if she was still pondering them as she and Joseph entered the Temple to make their offerings and consecrate Jesus to the Lord.

There will be many blessings spoken to you throughout your motherhood journey. There may also be words that "will pierce your own soul too." There will be Simeons to whom you will look for encouragement and enlightenment. They will faithfully offer you both, even though sometimes their words will unsettle your soul.

MOURNING INTO JOY

Julia, a friend of mine, has heard the message of the ancient Simeon ring through her own soul numerous times in recent years. She and her husband, Steve, are the parents of two beautiful healthy children, Michael and Rebekah. The angels didn't sing, and the magi didn't visit at their births; but the parents' hearts rejoiced, and God did indeed provide all their needs.

There will be many blessings spoken to you throughout your motherhood journey; there may also be words that will pierce your soul.

As the years passed after the birth of their second child, Julia longed to have more children. Finally, when Michael and Rebekah were 12 and 10, she received the good news that she was expecting again.

Their joy ended in an unexpected miscarriage. The loss of this new life was overwhelming, especially when it was learned that the child in the womb was not one but three—a set of triplets. Truly, a sword had pierced Julia's soul. Within the next year, healing came, and with it the news that she was expecting again.

Prior to the birth of this child, a question came to Julia's mind several times over a three-year period: Would you still be willing to have another baby if you knew something would be wrong with it? Believing this to be from the Lord because it produced no fear in her, she would conversationally respond, "Okay. But if You ask me to do this, I'm going to ask You for grace. I'll say yes because I believe that You only give good gifts."

Although this conversation went on in Julia's heart a number of times, she felt no fear throughout this pregnancy. Each time she prayed, the reassuring thought came to her, *I'm going to be with you.*

Due to an alarming dream prior to the birth of her new child, Julia and her husband made the decision to prepare Michael and Rebekah, now 14 and 12, for the possibility of the birth of a handicapped child. Both children wholeheartedly responded, "Mom, it doesn't matter. We will love the baby no matter what."

When the time of labor and delivery came, both Julia and her new baby girl almost died in the delivery process. Immediately after the birth of baby Elizabeth, the doctors and nurses quickly moved her to another room. Although Steve wanted to stay by Julia's side to watch over her, Julia sensed that her baby's life was in danger and insisted that Steve follow the doctors.

Tiny Elizabeth was simply not responding to life. Doctors and nurses filled the room in a panic of activity. When Steve asked if he could pray for his baby, the doctors stepped back, and within 30 seconds Elizabeth was breathing normally again. Stunned, the doctors and nurses stood with tear-filled eyes and wonder in their hearts for what seemed an eternal moment. This would be the first of many miracles in Elizabeth's life.

All babies have eight separate pieces of skull bone in their heads at the time of birth. The bones are separated to enable the baby to come through the birth canal successfully. One in 180,000 babies is born with one of these skull pieces fused. Baby Elizabeth had all eight bones fused together at the time of birth.

The doctor had broken little Elizabeth's skull during the birth process. Although this injury, plus the trauma of birth, put her life in immediate danger, it was the breaking of her skull that saved her life in the next few weeks. It also prevented her from being blind and mentally retarded, as the unyielding skull would have damaged the optic nerve and hindered the brain from developing normally.

It's amazing how God uses every "breaking" in our lives to release a miracle, both spiritually and naturally.

Although Julia was thankful for the new life God had placed into her hands, she was in shock in the hours following Elizabeth's birth. She recalls the feeling that even with the preparation God had given her, a person is never prepared for a severely deformed child.

The doctors were her Simeons. They began to tell her of their wonder at the miracle of Elizabeth's birth, yet they predicted the numerous surgeries that lay ahead for her. Julia went to sleep that first night thinking of the pain her little girl would have to face. In that moment, her heart was woven with Mary's when Mary had stood at the steps of the Temple and Simeon said, "A sword will pierce your own soul, too."

When Elizabeth was four days old, the doctor spoke to Steve and Julia about the first surgery she would need in just a few weeks. He had performed the surgery only once and knew of no other doctors in the nation who had ever done this kind of surgery. This was another sword in Julia's soul—a special child in her arms that no one really knew how to care for.

When Elizabeth was two weeks old, they took her to another specialist in another city to acquire a second opinion on the timing of the upcoming surgery. He agreed with the first doctor and even said, "I'd just take that skull off, throw it in the garbage and let her grow a new one." Julia was stunned at his seeming lack of care for the value of Elizabeth's life.

At 2:00 A.M. that morning, Julia picked up the *Gideon Bible* in the motel room and read, "As thou knowest not what is the way of the spirit, nor how the bones do grow in the womb of her that is with child: even so thou knowest not the works of God who maketh all" (Eccles. 11:5, *KJV*). Once again the gentle whispers of the Lord were engraved on her heart. Once again her faith was renewed. Just to be reminded that the Lord was Elizabeth's creator and He was watching over them restored her courage.

When Elizabeth was five weeks old, it was time for her first surgery. The night before the surgery, Julia cherished every moment with her baby, not knowing if Elizabeth would live through it. Julia recalls the hardest thing was when she handed the baby over to the doctors. Her only consolation was that in doing so, she was not merely handing Elizabeth over to a human doctor, but she was giving her into the hands of the Lord.

The doctors removed little Elizabeth's skull from her eyebrows to the back of her neck. It was a long nine-hour surgery. Although it was successful, she had another minor surgery only one week later. Elizabeth needed 24-hour monitoring. It was truly intensive care on the home front. Her life would be a constant blessing and challenge, not only to her mother but also to her entire family as they each participated in watching over her.

When it came time to officially present her to the Lord at a ceremony of dedication, Julia and Steve were well practiced in handing their daughter over to the Lord and into the hands of others. They did so with joy and anticipation of future miracles for this very special daughter.

When Elizabeth was 15 months old, the doctors needed to remove her complete skull so that the developing brain would have room to grow. This surgery was six months earlier than previously planned. Once again Julia found her emotions struggling with the piercing sword. "Oh, God, not more pain for Elizabeth. So soon? Why now?" This time Philippians 1:6 rang within her soul: "He who began a good work in you will carry it on to completion."

By now Elizabeth was walking. She would need to wear a helmet, following the surgery, to protect her head. Although her head was physically deformed, her intelligence was not; and she would not like the confinement of the helmet—another challenge for all involved. At a time of further extensive hospital testing and a minor surgery when Elizabeth was two and a half years old, the Lord graciously reassured Julia of His care. He then led her to the verse, "He that goeth forth and weepeth, bearing precious seed, shall doubtless come again with rejoicing, bringing his sheaves with him" (Ps. 126:6, *KJV*).

Elizabeth will face another surgery when she is five and again when she is six. She is a bright and intelligent child and is a delight to everyone who comes in contact with her. Oh yes, there are those who are initially shocked by her physical appearance, but then they meet with her winsome smile and can hardly resist giving a smile in return.

There were those who would also look upon Mary's child one day and proclaim, "He grew up before him like a tender shoot, and like a root out of dry ground. He had no beauty or majesty to attract us to him, nothing in his appearance that we should desire him" (Isa. 53:2). Yes, these two mothers—Mary and Julia—have been woven together in a great tapestry that reaches across the generations.

American poet Carl Sandburg once said, "A baby is God's opinion that the world should go on."[1] I think Mr. Sandburg is quite right. Every child should be "consecrated to the Lord," believed in and released to be who God has called him or her to be.

Regardless of how perfect or imperfect your child is according to the world's standards, you must continue to believe in him or her. When you falter in your courage, believe in the God who created your child and believe in the consecration you made.

In your motherhood journey, there may be days, months or years that a "sword will pierce your own soul too," but that doesn't mean life should stop for you or your child. It doesn't mean you should give up and walk away. Charles Spurgeon, speaking of a mother, once said, "She never quite leaves her children at home, even when she doesn't take them along."[2] What an incredibly true statement! Once you've started the journey, there's no turning back. Long before Mary consecrated her child, she consecrated herself, and that was what she held fast as she looked the future in the face.

Notes
1. *A Mother Is to Cherish* (Nashville: Thomas Nelson Publishers, 1994), n.p.
2. Ibid.

Chapter 7

TRUST FOR DAILY PROVISIONS

After Jesus was born in Bethlehem in Judea, during the time of King Herod, Magi from the east came to Jerusalem and asked, "Where is the one who has been born king of the Jews? We saw his star in the east and have come to worship him." When King Herod heard this he was disturbed, and all Jerusalem with him. After they had heard the king, they went on their way, and the star they had seen in the east went ahead of them until it stopped over the place where the child was. When they saw the star, they were overjoyed. On coming to the house, they saw the child with his mother Mary, and they bowed down and worshipped him. Then they opened their treasures and presented him with gifts of gold and of incense and of myrrh. And having been warned in a dream not to go back to Herod, they returned to their country by another route. When they had gone, an angel of the Lord appeared to Joseph in a dream. "Get up," he said, "take the child and his mother and escape to Egypt. Stay there until I tell you, for Herod is going to search for the child to kill him." So he got up, took the child and his mother during the night and left for Egypt, where he stayed until the death of Herod.

MATTHEW 2:1-3,9-15

Who was this entourage of magi just leaving Herod's palace? Where had they come from and where were they going? What did these Gentiles know that others didn't?

It was obvious to anyone who knew anything that Herod was declining in health and aging quickly. Augustus was also advanced in years, and since the retirement of Tiberius, Rome had been without an experienced military commander. In fact, Phraates IV of Parthia was a very unpopular and aging king himself. The Persian Parthians did have leaders who had Jewish blood running through their veins. Could it be that these men from the East had a new king in view? Was it for Rome, for Persia or, perhaps, for another nation?

The word on the streets was that they had told Herod they were following a star and looking for "the one who has been born king of the Jews." What an obvious, calculated insult to Herod. How would he take it? What would he do? Could he be bothered by their questions, or would he have the horses cinched up and the chariots ready to go for a ride soon?

Could it be that God was using a supernatural star to lead these magi out of their heathen land? Perhaps they had read Balaam's prophecy: "I see him, but not now; I behold him, but not near. A star will come out of Jacob; a scepter will rise out of Israel" (Num. 24:17). After all, in days past He had led His people out of Egypt by a pillar of cloud by day and a pillar of fire by night (see Exod. 13:21).

In addition to all the rumors, every knowledgeable Jew knew that Daniel's prophecy would soon come to pass, but what would Herod do if he realized it? What did he know? What did these magi know? Who were they looking for and where were they going?

Little did the populace of Jerusalem realize that by the time they were done talking about the entourage from the East, the magi would have traveled on to Bethlehem and departed again. Bethlehem was only six miles from Jerusalem—a relatively easy traveling distance for this gift-bearing group. They would be the first Gentiles to pay homage to the Christ child but not the last. They were only the first among many who would bow their knee to Him.

I wonder what Mary's thoughts were in the days following that noted visit.

Here I am again, Lord. Thank You for answering my prayers. You knew that Joseph was getting concerned about our finances, and then these magi show up! Wow! And again I say, Wow!

Who were they anyway, and where did they come from? Okay, okay. I'm only on a need-to-know basis, I know. Thank You for Your provisions. I proclaim with Jeremiah of old, "Yet this I call to mind and therefore I have hope: Because of the LORD'S great love we are not consumed, for his compassions never fail. They are new every morning; great is Your faithfulness" (Lam. 3:21-23).

Joseph tells me that he's had a dream of impending doom and he's sure it's from You. So again, we must go. Help me to know what to pack and what to leave. You will protect us, I know. Do watch over our child; He is dearer to me than life itself.

The psalmist said, "Praise be to the Lord, to God our Savior, who daily bears our burdens. Our God is a God who saves; from the Sovereign LORD comes escape from death" (Ps. 68:19,20). Let it be so, Father.

Thank You for Your abundant provisions—the gifts to bring money and the dreams to bring refuge. What is that You are whispering in my ear, Lord? This is preparation for the future? This time I will be able to protect Him, but there's coming a day when I will not be able to? What are these thoughts? Are these

from You? I must tuck these away and ponder them on my pil-
low. I trust You, Father. I yield to You.

This time, Mary would be able to find a place of refuge for her
baby, but there was coming a day when there would be no provision for Him but a cross. The Gentile magi came with money
that would provide temporary refuge, and gifts that symbolized
His life and death as an offering to God. Although these Gentiles
would be the first to proclaim Him as King of the Jews, there
would be another Gentile, named Pilate, who would be the last
to do so in this time period; and he would proclaim it through a
placard on a cross.

Egypt, the land that had once represented bondage and
oppression to Jews, was now a place of refuge and safety for
Mary and her son. The very land in which her descendants had
suffered under the heavy hand of ungodly Egyptian kings would
now be a land of safety. Their stay in Egypt would be adequately
financed by the unexpected gifts of the magi who did not know
their God.

How sad that Herod, a Jewish king who should have known
and understood the Old Testament prophecies, did not person-
ally search for this new young king to properly honor Him. How
glorious that these Gentile magi did seek and honor Him. How
strange and yet how wonderful that God's provision came to
Mary and Joseph from unexpected people in unexpected ways.

Have there ever been times in your mothering that you were
in great need of God's miraculous provision? Have there ever
been times when you needed a place of refuge as well as food on
the table?

God's provision comes in a variety of ways. It comes when
we're watching and waiting, and it comes when we least expect it.
It comes when we've worked hard to be a part of the provision and

when we've done nothing to deserve it. God wants us to feel secure, but He loves to surprise us. Truly, He is a most wonderful provider.

A DREAM FULFILLED

Marion was from western Canada. She and her husband had purchased a six-acre farm with the intention of subdividing and selling it in the future. He was developing his own business when he unexpectedly died, leaving Marion with little financial security for her and her children, ages two and four.

Four years after her husband's death, she met the Lord Jesus as her personal Savior and her heart began to burn with desire for Bible training and the mission field. In the eyes of most people, being a young widow and the mother of two and living on a limited budget would have been overwhelming obstacles. But not to Marion. They were simply challenges she needed to continually yield to her loving heavenly Father.

She was an energetic and intelligent woman, but how would she fulfill this new desire consuming

God's provision comes in a variety of ways. It comes when we're watching and waiting and when we least expect it.

her heart? Her friends wondered, her daughters trusted, and she listened to the Father's voice.

As a widow, Marion received $40 a month from the government for financial aid. She sold eggs, milk and fruit from the land to make ends meet. She also learned how to raise calves and have them butchered.

Several years later she even got a part-time job doing bookkeeping. She sewed and did her best to shop wisely at second-hand stores to clothe her daughters. The girls got a new pair of shoes twice each year for their growing feet and a new coat every two years.

After her salvation experience, Marion immediately began to tithe what little she had. Her butchered calves became her tithe for a season. She trusted God and His ability to provide, more than she trusted her own ability to budget. Her theme verse during this period in her life was "Trust in the LORD with all your heart and lean not on your own understanding; in all your ways acknowledge him, and he will make your paths straight" (Prov. 3:5,6).

She and her daughters prayed together every day for God to provide. Then with grateful hearts they thanked Him for His provision. Her oldest daughter recalls, "God always provided enough. We never went hungry. In fact, [my sister and I] didn't realize we were 'poor' until we got older."

When Marion's daughters were ages 13 and 11, she was prompted by the Lord to sell the farm and move to the United States to attend Bible college and see what the Lord would do. Her plan was to stretch out her college education to seven years so that her youngest child could finish high school in the same location.

As an international college student, she was only permitted to work 20 hours a week. However, the sale of the property provided enough money on a monthly basis to pay their rent, her college fees and her daughters' school fees. This lasted four years before the new owner of the farm passed away and his heirs stopped payment on the land.

Now what would she do? She trusted the Lord and did her part, and He did His. Again her theme song was "Trust in the Lord with all your heart and lean not on your own understanding." As she trusted, God did one little miracle after another. I don't know if America is an appropriate likeness to Egypt, but I do know that God blessed this faithful mother and took care of her and her children in a foreign land.

One year after her return to her homeland, the farmland was turned back into her hands and she was able to resell it. Today she administrates a Christian overseas correspondence school for her local church. She also writes Bible curriculum for students who live in other nations and are hungry for sound doctrine and Bible teaching.

Her eldest daughter is married and travels with her husband around the world for the purpose of winning the lost to Christ through the avenue of drama evangelism. She is also one of the executive secretaries of a large church in Portland, Oregon. Her youngest daughter is a high school English teacher in Canada and spends her summers teaching English in overseas nations.

Is this mother's dream being fulfilled? Was her trust in God to provide daily for her and her daughters worthy of her trust? Yes! Not only is she fulfilling her dream of reaching a mission field, her seed is multiplied and she is touching many through her writing as well as through her daughters' lives.

Like Mary, this mother was on a journey that would take her to a near-distant land. To succeed, she would need to be brave, trusting and wise. Her provisions for the journey would be minimal but adequate. Her seeds of trust have been multiplied many times over. God's daily provision has been abundant beyond anything she could ever imagine.

A wise man—some attribute this to Charles Spurgeon— once said, "Do not carve your name on a tree or a wall, write it on the heart of a little child." What you leave in your child will always be more important than what you leave to them.

You may not be a widow and you may not have an insecure Eastern tyrant searching for your children with the intention of slaying them. However, we all need to trust the Lord at times for provision, both in our mothering and for our children.

Did you ever feel helpless when your child was being bullied or mocked by his or her peers? Did you ever shed a tear when your child forgot the notes in the middle of a music recital or missed the goal in the championship soccer match? Did you ever feel like spending more money than your budget would allow for the sake of a pair of shoes or jeans with a label on it? Did you ever wonder why God seems to bless some people more than others?

If you've done any of these things, maybe it's not an escape to Egypt you need. Maybe it's a respite in God's presence. What is my recommendation? Tie a knot in your emotional rope and hang on; God has a blessing for you on the other end.

It won't be long before you'll be pondering questions like these: Did you ever cry when you heard your daughter sing the national anthem at a basketball game? Did you ever wipe away a tear when your son testified in youth camp at the beginning of the week when all the other campers still had bad attitudes? Did you ever silently rejoice when your child gave all of his or her hard-earned money to a poor family at Christmas? Did you ever maintain your composure on the outside but shout on the inside, *Yes! That's my kid!* Did you ever just stop and thank God for His marvelous, miraculous, amazing daily provisions?

Chapter 8

A MOTHER'S FORMATIVE INFLUENCE

When Joseph and Mary had done everything required by the Law of the Lord,
they returned to Galilee to their own town of Nazareth. And the child
grew and became strong; he was filled with wisdom, and the
grace of God was upon him.

LUKE 2:39,40

Every good Jewish home was the center of religious training in the early years of a young boy's life. But Mary wanted more for Jesus than the simple memorization of Scripture reading and writing. Didn't Solomon say, "The fear of the Lord is the beginning of knowledge.... Listen, my son, to your father's instruction and do not forsake your mother's teaching" (Prov. 1:7,8)? She must impart these truths to little Jesus as well. Where, oh where, should she begin?

Mary must have felt somewhat overwhelmed by the responsibility set before her. She knew when Gabriel came to her that he was asking something big of her. She knew that her trust in the Father's guidance would have to deepen in her spirit. Upon receiving this actual life into her care, I wonder if one of her conversations with God went something like this:

You really did it, Father. You really placed the life of this supernatural, yet completely natural, child in my arms. My heart is overwhelmed. "I call on you, O God, for you will answer me; give ear to me and hear my prayer" (Ps. 17:6).

Lord, as Isaiah of old said, please give me "an instructed tongue" (Isa. 50:4). Waken me morning by morning; waken my ear to listen like one being taught. Sovereign Lord, who "wakens my ear to listen" (Isa. 50:5), open my ears that I might know what to say and what to do. Make me a mother who can discern the questions of His spirit and the intents of His heart. Cause me to imprint on His spirit that which You have destined.

Where do I begin? You are so amazing and He is so precious! Oh, is that where I begin—with "amazing" and "precious"? Yes, Lord, I'll begin there.

Have you ever looked at your child and felt overwhelmed at the obvious responsibility before you? Have you ever assessed how many of your own mother's qualities you do and do not personify, and then wondered how many of your own qualities your child will show?

I can remember the first parent-teacher conference my husband and I had with one of our children's first teachers. She complimented us on the child. (Attention all mothers! That's the warm-up.) Then as she continued to discuss our child's artwork and classroom habits, after each assessment she contemplatively said, "And I don't know why your child does that." Each time she made that statement, my husband and I took turns looking at each other with eyes that said, "That's you! You're the reason for that one!"

The session was brief, but it seemed like a 48-hour emotional undressing, layer by layer. We walked out of that parent-teacher conference convinced that parenting was going to give us much more "exposure" than we ever imagined. Although this teacher never openly pointed a finger at us and said "You are the cause," we both knew that our little charge was definitely affected by us, for better or worse. What an unexpected and rude awakening!

THE RESULT OF PERSEVERING INFLUENCE

I have a wonderful friend who is a pastor's wife. She and her husband are very vibrant, godly people who have done their best to serve the Lord together for many years. When their bouncing blond-haired, blue-eyed baby boy came along, they couldn't have been happier. They already had one other child a few years older, and things were going just fine. But this new little fellow definitely had a mind of his own.

When he was four years old, he had at home a set of Bible storybooks from which his mother and father read to him on a regular basis. During one phase of this season, he became especially intrigued with the story in the book of Daniel about the three Hebrew children who were thrown into the fiery furnace. At the same time he was also very interested in the concept of hell and how people could end up there.

He regularly attended children's church on Sunday mornings. Of course, since he was the associate pastor's son, he had no real options. He was energetic, curious by nature and usually somewhat mischievous during children's church. One day he was particularly disruptive. His blond hair and sparkling blue eyes were not going to help him escape discipline this day. The teachers collectively decided to place him on a chair in the corner, facing the wall. As soon as they resumed teaching, the little tyke stood up on his chair and began to yell at the teachers in front of the whole group, "You are all going to burn in hell for putting me in this corner!"

For the rest of the year, on Sundays he sat with his mother on the front row of church. His "children's church" was near her side in the "big people's" church service.

While administrating a summertime vacation Bible school two years later, this young mother once again came to grips with the extremes to which her six-year-old would go. She was extremely busy with all of the details of her job description for the week—coordinating teachers, class locations, crafts, refreshments and a variety of other details.

One day, one of her son's teachers, looking rather sheepish and embarrassed, came to her and said, "I'm sure this probably isn't true, but your son has just requested special prayer for you and your husband. He says he's unable to go to sleep at night because you guys are up until two in the morning every night screaming at each other and fighting." Then the teacher looked at her and said, "Is there a problem that we need to know about? Can we help in any way?"

The son's accusation was a lie, and it put his mother and his teacher in an embarrassing place. Did this young mother need to impart her sense of appropriateness to her son? Yes, she did. Did she need the ability to assess a situation and wait for the suitable time to address it? Most definitely. Did her future hold some challenges with this bright, quick-witted child? Yes, it did.

Today this son is a fine young man who is serving the Lord and only has accolades for his parents, as they do for him. He's now married and doing great. There's no more deceit or false predictions in his mouth. They made it through, this mother and son, because she, like Mary, held on to the hope that was within her and took the time to mold and influence him for Christ in his formative years.

A MOTHER'S INFLUENCE

Jesus' education, under Mary's tutelage, would have begun at the age of three with much memorization of Scripture. Between the ages of five and ten he would have learned to read and write and study the Scripture.

The household duties of the Jewish mother included "grinding flour, cooking, laundry, making beds, and spinning wool. She was also supposed to maintain an attractive appearance for her husband. The husband was required to provide her with food and clothing, maintain regular sexual relations, provide for the children, and was forbidden to strike her. The woman's influence in the family was considered greater than the man's."[1]

Needless to say, Mary had her work cut out for her. As a mother, she had specific responsibilities outlined by her culture, including the responsibility and duty to impart her upbringing and the Scriptures to her children. I have a suspicion that Mary did it with joy as well.

Even though in our contemporary culture we may not find ourselves grinding flour or spinning wool apart from specific nutritional desires or the sheer novelty of it, we do still have a responsibility to impart the Word of God and Spirit of Christ to our children. It is through imparting Christ that security, emotional stability and healthy citizenry will grow in our children.

WHEN APPROVAL IS WITHHELD
Evangelist Kathryn Kuhlman once said, "I can never remember, as a child, having my mother show me any affection. Never. Mama was a perfect disciplinarian. But she never once told me she was proud of me or that I did well. Never once. It was Papa who gave me the love and affection."[2] Her biographer wrote:

> After Kathryn became famous, she used to get on the phone at night and call her mother back in Concordia, talking for hours at a time. According to the telephone operator, Kathryn was constantly trying to prove to her mother that she had succeeded. "She would giggle and giggle," the former operator told me, "and of course we'd sit there listening and giggle too. Then she would tell her mother all she had gotten: 'Mama, I've got the biggest Christmas tree in the city. It's sooooo tall, and has more than 5,000 lights on it.' She would talk about the size of the offering at her miracle services as if she was trying to convince her mother that she was a success."[3]

What a sad narrative. I'm sure that Kathryn's mother loved her. But her inability to impart that love to her daughter early in her life left Kathryn in need of constant reassurance of her acceptance. Sadly, it also left her insecurity exposed to prying eyes and listening ears.

THE HALLMARK OF A MOTHER'S LOVE

Corrie Ten Boom, well-known speaker and heroine of the anti-Nazi underground, had a different experience with her mother.

> Mama could have coffee on the stove and a cake in the oven as fast as most people could say "best wishes." And since she knew almost everyone in Harlem, especially the poor, sick and neglected, there was almost no day in the year that was not for somebody, as she would say with eyes shining, "a very special occasion!"[4]

I wonder if it was through this impartation that Corrie received the grace and kindness to give to the poor, sick and neglected later in life. She tells in the end of her autobiography:

> It was at a church service in Munich that I saw him, the former SS man who had stood guard at the shower room door in the processing center at Ravensbruck. He was the first of our actual jailers that I had seen since that time. And suddenly it was all there—the roomful of mocking men, the heaps of clothing, Betsie's pain-blanched face.
>
> He came up to me as the church was emptying, beaming and bowing. "How grateful I am for your message, Fraulein," he said. "To think that, as you say, He has washed my sins away!"
>
> His hand was thrust out to shake mine. And I, who had preached so often to the people in Bloemendaal the need to forgive, kept my hand at my side.
>
> Even as the angry, vengeful thoughts boiled through me, I saw the sin of them. Jesus Christ had died for this man; was I going to ask for more? *Lord Jesus, I prayed, forgive me and help me to forgive him.*

I tried to smile, I struggled to raise my hand. I could not. I felt nothing, not the slightest spark of warmth or charity. And so again I breathed a silent prayer. *Jesus, I cannot forgive him. Give me Your forgiveness.*

As I took his hand the most incredible thing happened. From my shoulder along my arm and through my hand a current seemed to pass from me to him, while into my heart sprang a love for this stranger that almost overwhelmed me.

And so I discovered that it is not on our forgiveness any more than on our goodness that the world's healing hinges, but on His. When He tells us to love our enemies, He gives, along with the command, the love itself.[5]

Yes, it was both Christ's forgiveness and the compassion of Corrie's mother for the poor, sick and neglected that had graced her own life with supernatural love for this enemy. The SS officer had left an indelible mark on Corrie's soul, not one that was easily forgiven. This was a pivotal point in her life, and as she reached out to Christ, He reached back to her. In an instant, a firebrand touched her heart, healed her wounds and imparted love itself.

From this time on, she was free to impart that same grace, not only to the wounded she identified with, but also to the wounded beyond her natural ability to love—whom Christ died for as well.

MODELING A KIND SPIRIT

There are so many unsung heroines among the long list of mothers throughout the ages. I must tell you of one more who imparted much to her daughter. This mother's name was Drana

Bojaxhiu. She came from a large, well-established family in Prizren, Albania. She was known to be gentle, engaging, generous and full of compassion toward the poor.

She became a widow and was left with three children to raise. Their ages were fifteen, eleven and eight. To support the family after the death of her husband, she embroidered and made bridal dresses and costumes for various festivals.

No matter how little she had, she always had something to give to the poor. Her youngest daughter, Agnes, said, "Never did anyone go away empty-handed. Every day at table something was left for the poor. The first time, I asked my mother, 'Who are they?' She replied: 'Some are relatives; the others are our own people.' When I grew up I understood that these were the poor people who had nothing, but whom my mother fed."[6]

Drana often told her children, "When you do good, do it as if you were casting a stone into the depth of the sea."

Agnes says of her family memories, "Ours was a happy family, full of joy, of love, and of happy children."[7]

Agnes Bojaxhiu is known to most today as Mother Teresa, who spent many years of her life in India. She opened several refuges for the dying, especially those with leprosy. She also started many orphanages for abandoned children and orphans. She trained others to care for the poor, and she affected our generation with the love of Christ. It was commonly known that at 85 years of age she slept only three to four hours a night and prayed five hours a day.

When seeking the Lord concerning her call to the mission field as a young woman, she said that she could hear in her heart her mother's words: "When you take on a task, do it willingly; otherwise, do not accept it."[8]

Yes, her mother's spirit and her words would ring in Agnes's ears for many years to come. That impartation would help carry her into the presence of the poor, diseased and dying; earthly kings and presidents; and ultimately the King of kings.

REAPING WHAT YOU SOW

Whether you feed the poor, make tea for your neighbors or give grace to an enemy, know that your children are watching and receiving. They will receive more from your example than you'll probably ever fully realize. But it will be obvious one day when you take a good long look at your grandchildren. Much of what we impart to our children will be passed on to another generation, for better or for worse.

Don't be afraid; remember the promise: "He gently leads those that have young" (Isa. 40:11). So cling to His leading, and watch "the child grow and become strong; filled with wisdom, and the grace of God" (Luke 2:40).

Whether you feed the poor, make tea for your neighbors or give grace to an enemy, know that your children are watching and receiving your example.

Notes
1. Everett Ferguson, *Backgrounds of Early Christianity* (Grand Rapids, Mich.: William B. Eerdmans, 1993), p. 71.

2. Jamie Buckingham, *Daughter of Destiny, Kathryn Kuhlman . . . Her Story* (Plainfield, N.J.: Logos International, 1976), p. 15.

3. Ibid., p. 16.

4. Corrie Ten Boom, *The Hiding Place* (New York: Bantam Books, 1971), p. 6.

5. Ibid., p. 238

6. Lush Gjergji, *Mother Teresa: Her Life, Her Works* (New York: New City Press, 1991), p. 15.

7. Ibid., p. 16.

8. Ibid., p. 12.

THE STAGES OF RELEASE

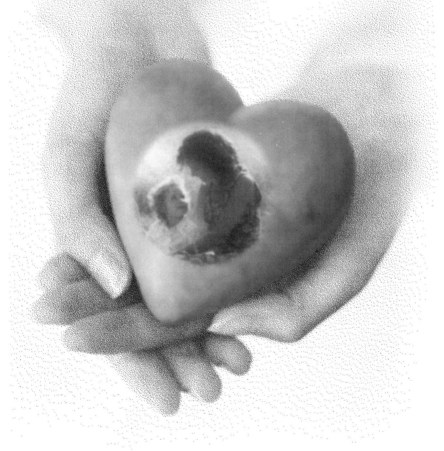

Chapter 9

RELEASING INTO ADOLESCENCE

Every year his parents went to Jerusalem for the Feast of the Passover. When he was twelve years old, they went up to the Feast, according to the custom. After the Feast was over, while his parents were returning home, the boy Jesus stayed behind in Jerusalem, but they were unaware of it. Thinking he was in their company, they traveled on for a day. Then they began looking for him among their relatives and friends. When they did not find him, they went back to Jerusalem to look for him. After three days they found him in the temple courts, sitting among the teachers, listening to them and asking them questions. Everyone who heard him was amazed at his understanding and his answers. When his parents saw him, they were astonished. His mother said to him, "Son, why have you treated us like this? Your father and I have been anxiously searching for you."

"Why were you searching for me?" he asked. "Didn't you know I had to be in my Father's house?" But they did not understand what he was saying to them. Then he went down to Nazareth with them and was obedient to them. But his mother treasured all these things in her heart.

LUKE 2:41-51

Going to Jerusalem every year was a blessing, even though it was at least a three-day journey. This year had been especially meaningful because Jesus was old enough to become a son of the Law. This meant that He was now considered an adult member of the Jewish community and was obligated to keep the Law. The ceremony had been so special, but now Mary and Joseph were totally distracted from the joys of the feast because Jesus was missing.

Jerusalem was full of people at this time of the year. Where would they find him? Joseph had assumed that Jesus was traveling with Mary and the other women and children. Mary had assumed that because Jesus had stepped into His first level of adulthood as a young man, He must be traveling with Joseph and the other men. Terror struck their hearts when they discovered that neither of them had seen Jesus in quite a long time. What if He was harmed? What if they couldn't find Him?

Oh Father, He's gone! You entrusted Him into our care and He's gone! How could we be so careless? How could He be so mindless? He knows that Jerusalem's streets are not always safe during feast times. Why didn't He stay close to us like He knew to do? When He was small He would always hold tightly to my hand, but not anymore. After all, now He's twelve and a son of the Law. But Father, He's still my boy. I know He's older, but there are so many people who might do Him harm. He knows better than to do this. How could He not be more careful? He's so trusting, so inquisitive, so unprepared for the real world. Oh, Father, please protect Him; please watch over Him.

Have you ever felt as if your teenagers were just a step ahead of where you wanted them to be in social independence? Have you ever thought they were in one place and then discovered they were in another? Have you ever wondered about the company they were keeping or if they were wise enough to realize when they were in danger? Have you ever rebuked them and then wondered if you handled the situation in the right way? Have you ever gone out of your way to make a celebration special for them only to discover their focus was elsewhere?

All of these questions and more must have gone through Mary's mind that day. Nazareth was approximately 70 miles from Jerusalem, and it was not uncommon for large numbers of families to travel together to and from the feasts. It was also not uncommon for the women and small children, who traveled more slowly, to begin the journey home before the men, who would catch up to them by evening and set up camp for the night.

It's easy to understand how Jesus wasn't missed immediately. The reference to three days in this passage of Scripture probably refers to a day's journey away from Jerusalem, a day's journey back and a day of searching for Him in the city. Obviously, as soon as they realized Jesus was not with either of them, they returned to the city to search for Him.

Although all Jewish men within a certain radius of Jerusalem were required to attend the feasts, the women were not. However, Mary made a special effort to attend. This was a special year—the year that Jesus would become a son of the Law. Little did Mary know that for her, this trip would bring about the second stage of release of her firstborn son.

The Temple was not just a center for prayer, consecration and sacrifice; it was also a place for teaching. It was customary for the Sanhedrin to meet in public in the Temple court to discuss religious and theological questions. The Jewish teachers enjoyed conducting classes during feast times in the Temple courts.

Asking questions was a common mode of learning. In fact, the rabbis enjoyed being asked questions, not only to instruct, but also to show off their great knowledge. The only stipulation to the questions was that they be intelligent.

The passage of Scripture in Luke 2:47 indicates that Jesus' questions and responses were indeed intelligent and perceptive. The passage actually says that teachers were "amazed at his understanding and his answers." Although Jesus didn't perform any miracles here, the Greek text indicates that the teachers knew they were in the presence of a young man who was more than just a brilliant young student. They recognized the wisdom of God resting on Him. Luke had already noted in verse 40 that the grace of God was upon Jesus; this must have been apparent to His teachers in this setting as well.

Have you ever been amazed at insightful statements and perceptions made by your young teenagers? Has it ever seemed to you that one minute they act immature and the next minute they make some profound statement that goes over your head?

I can remember more than once being amazed by my teens when they shared with me a word of counsel they had given to a friend. The thoughts were beyond their years of understanding. I can also remember being amazed at how my son could administrate a clean-up crew after a party; and I always marveled at his ability to work and program all the electronic gadgets around the house.

I can also recall the first time I heard my teen daughter practicing a piano piece that went beyond my own skills, and memorizing and reciting the book of Proverbs in its entirety. I could go on and on with examples. (The wonder of a mother's memories is entertaining to her children but boring to most!) I'm sure your teens have demonstrated certain perceptions and talents that have amazed you as well.

When Mary and Joseph found Jesus in the Temple, Mary spoke to Him as though He were a child. (Any mother of a child in middle school knows this is a big mistake.) Mary actually rebuked Him for what she considered to be insensitivity on His part. In so many words, she told Him, "You have acted like a child." Her joy in finding Him was clouded by the frustration and anxiety she had experienced.

The commandment to honor one's father and mother was regarded by the Jews as one of the most important of all the laws. Children who were not yet considered to be adults were to express this honor, in part, by their obedience to their parents. It is here that Mary met with her second release. She spoke to Jesus as though He were a child, even though He had just become a recognized adult in the Jewish community. From Him she received a gentle but firm and surprising response.

When Mary said, "Your father and I . . . ," Jesus gently and precisely responded by taking the title of father from Joseph and giving it to God.

History doesn't tell us if Jesus was aware of His deity prior to this. However, from this point on, He obviously knew who His Father was. His deity was now a spoken revelation to Him and His mother, even though He may not have known all that it entailed at this point. Although Scripture says that Mary and Joseph did not understand what Jesus was saying, I'm sure they took it to heart and pondered it in the days ahead.

A DELICATE BALANCE OF RELEASE

If you have teens in your household, what have you been pondering lately? Are the rules and regulations of your household clear or do they change from day to day? Do you speak to your teen in the same manner in which you spoke to him or her in childhood days? Do you find your-self making a transition from instant-obedience-without-ques-tion to "come now, let us reason together" (Isa. 1:18)? Has your style of discipline become a confusing issue for both you and your teen?

I can remember when a wise Elizabeth said to me in one of my moments of frustration and ques-tioning: "You have to discern between true rebellion and the 'lit-tle man' inside." She continued to explain to me that, especially with a son, a mother is the first woman he practices his leadership skills on. What a revelation!

It is important that in moments of the seeming need for discipline that you discern between immatu-rity and disobedience, between "practice" and rebellion. It's a pre-carious tightrope to walk. But if we assume that every disagreement is willful disrespect or disregard for our leadership as a parent, we may be missing the mark, especially with our sons.

There is a delicate balance of release in the teen years. Some par-ents hold on so tightly that their teens rebel against the parents'

Even though the events and moods in teens' lives can vary as much as the hairs on their heads, learn to ride the emotional ups and downs with grace and compassion rather than reaction and resentment.

authority and guidance. They feel smothered and unable to grow, so they break away. Other parents let go of their teens to such an extreme that the teens feel unloved and bereft of genuine care. They feel lost in a maze in which they have no sense of mature guidance. They want direction but have been left to discover it for themselves.

Most of us are somewhere in between these two extremes, and it still feels precarious at times. Even though the events and moods in a teen's life can vary as much as the hairs on their heads, doing your best to enjoy the parenting adventure at every stage of your child's life will only benefit your posture in this new season of release. Learn to ride the emotional ups and downs with grace and compassion rather than reaction and resentment.

There is no specific or set pattern for parenting your teens. Each child is an individual and has a specific blueprint for each season of his or her growth. But we can take a cue of release from Mary. Notice that after she and Jesus had this encounter, she did not further rebuke Him, and He came home for what is known as the 18 "silent years" of His life.

I'm sure that in this instance she must have been startled by His response. I'm sure she must have felt a bit confused, perhaps even resentful. Yet she obviously quickly postured herself to receive revelation from the Father for this moment in their lives.

I think the key to successfully releasing your teen is to maintain a humble posture before the Lord and not insist that your role assumes correctness. You'll be amazed at how often God will bless the "little man" (or "little woman") and allow them to be right, even if their attitude or perception is not correct.

You will also be amazed at how God will cover you and anoint your role as a parent, even when you are wrong or do not display the attitude He would desire from you. God will always stand by you in your parental position. He has ordained it to be so. However, discernment is important. For God warns parents: "Do not exasperate your children; instead bring them up in the training and instruction of the Lord" (Eph.6:4).

RELEASING YOUR TEENS FOR THEIR GOOD

Just as, I am sure, Mary felt anxiety about releasing her obviously strong-minded, perceptive young teen at this season, there was another mother in history who must have had similar emotions about releasing her young teen. She was the mother of the famous poet and hymn writer Fanny Crosby. Although this woman's husband died before Fanny was even 12 months old, she lived past 91.

When Fanny was six weeks old, she caught a slight cold that caused an inflammation in her eyes. The family physician was out of town, so Fanny's mother called another doctor. He recommended a remedy that destroyed little Fanny's eyesight.

This is what Fanny wrote of him in her autobiography:

> But I have not for a moment, in more than eighty-five years, felt a spark of resentment against him, because I have always believed from my youth to this very moment that the good Lord, in his infinite mercy, by this means, consecrated me to the work that I am still permitted to do. When I remember his mercy and lovingkindness; when I have been blessed above the common lot of mortals; and when happiness has touched the deep places of my soul, how can I repine?[1]

There is no doubt that Fanny's Presbyterian mother and grandmother influenced her mind-set in this regard. Fanny had a love for life and for Christ. Her attitude is reflected in this personal statement: "It has always been my favorite theory that the blind can accomplish nearly everything that may be done by those who can see. Do not think that those who are deprived of physical vision are shut out from the best that earth has to offer her children."[2]

Fanny grew up in the country, about which she says, "To a young and imaginative person there is nothing more inspiring than life in the country. Existence becomes a perpetual dream of delight; and there are no pangs to sadden the buoyant spirit."[3] However, with all that the country and the local village school had to offer her, she longed to know more. She often prayed for the Lord to show her how she could learn like other children.

The answer to the prayer of her heart, and the release from her mother, arrived on the same day when she was almost 15 years old. She says that as her mother read the letter of acceptance from the New York Institution for the Blind, she clapped her hands and exclaimed, "Oh, thank God, He has answered my prayer, just as I knew He would." Fanny continues in her autobiography, "That was the happiest day of my life; for the dark intellectual maze in which I had been living seemed to yield to hope and the promise of the light that was about to dawn.... The New York Institution was a foreign name to me, but it was enough to know that some place existed where I might be taught; and my star of promise even then was becoming a great orb of light."[4]

In her personal story she adds,

My mother was fully conscious of my joy, but to test me she said, "What will you do without me? You have never been away from home for more than two weeks at one time in your whole life." This presented a new idea: I had not thought of the separation from her; and for a moment I wavered. Then I answered as bravely as I could, "Much as I love you, Mother, I am willing to make any sacrifice to acquire an education." And she replied, "You are right, my child, and I am very glad you have the chance to go." But her voice betrayed the tremor in her heart. How wonderful is a mother's love. [5]

I'm sure this mother's release was a challenging one, for she had no husband to console her, and she had been the sole caretaker of Fanny for nearly 15 years. Although she would remain at home alone, she had rewarding years ahead. Truly, love brings about a fruit-bearing release.

Although Fanny had written poetry from the time she was a child, she didn't write her first hymn until she was 44 years old. From that time on, until she died, she wrote almost 9,000 hymns, often three within a week's time. Among them are such well-known hymns as "Blessed Assurance," "All the Way My Savior Leads Me" and "Rescue the Perishing."

Fanny could quote the entire Pentateuch, all four Gospels, Proverbs, Ruth, Song of Solomon and part of the book of Psalms. She often said that her goal was to lead one million people to Christ before she died. She died at the age of 95. One has to wonder if, through her hymns, she accomplished her goal.

A mother's release of her teen is emotionally challenging and sacrificial. It requires trust in the Lord and in that which she has already imparted to the child. Is it significant and potentially fruitful? Most definitely.

RELEASING YOUR TEEN TO GOD

There is another mother I know who released her teen in a different way. Night after night she watched her teen come home with a troubled countenance. She would ask him a few questions about his day but received little response. She was, as many mothers are in this season, reduced to prayer. There are no more attentive ears than the ones that listen to a mother's prayers.

This mother could not easily discern her son's personal quandary. He was a star athlete and at the top of his class academically, and he played an instrument in a lead position in the school band. Not only did he have all of these accomplishments going for him, he was also respected by his teachers and had friends who were true buddies and girls who were easily flattered by his attention.

Even though the Lord had favored him with all of these wonderful blessings, she noticed that he rarely seemed happy, especially at church. He had received Christ as his personal Savior when he was a young child. As a teen, he was obedient and honored his parents by attending services, but his heart wasn't in it. When she tried to draw him out, her son was polite but withdrawn from any family conversation that had any genuine depth.

One night, when they had out-of-town overnight guests in their home, he came in around ten o'clock in the evening and then left again within a few minutes "to go for a walk." She had noticed his troubled countenance as he came and left, but she attempted to remain focused on her guests. After they went to bed, she went to prayer. As she prayed, she sensed the Lord's assurance that her son was in His hands and that he would return, not only physically but spiritually as well. She went to bed trusting not in her son but in her Lord.

She didn't know how deeply entrenched her son was in a double-standard lifestyle, appearing one way to his parents and another to his friends at school. She didn't know how this pattern was replacing his faith with confusion and pain. She didn't know that if she had pressed him on the concerns of his heart he would have left. She had no awareness of the self-destructive behavior he was engaged in. She didn't know that he was seriously contemplating suicide that dark and lonely night. But she did know the God she had dedicated her son to many years prior. Yes, her confidence rested in God, not in her son.

The main key to successfully releasing your teen is to release the teen and embrace the Master.

Within a few days, a beloved aunt and uncle came to visit. The aunt, who was endeared to the teen, and a praying woman herself, had a very insightful conversation with her nephew. The Lord had revealed to her in prayer the young man's struggles. Not long after their conversation, this teenager made a distinct turnaround and made clear choices to follow the Lord.

Did this young man's mother need to release her teen even when she wanted to hold him more tightly? Yes. Did she need to release him to seek and find God for himself in this tenuous season of his life? Yes. Was it hard? Did it create anxious moments within her own spirit? Was it scary? Yes to all of the above. Was there any other way? Probably not. Eventually, he would need to find God for himself.

Did this son already know his mother's perspective on the issues he was struggling with? Yes. This was part of his greatest struggle. Would he, at this point, have listened to her repeat to him the values she held most dear? Yes, but he wouldn't have accepted it. Did he want to hurt and disappoint her? Most assuredly not. Did he desperately need and even want her prayers? Most definitely, even when he struggled against them as an unbroken stallion resists the master's corral. Would he have made it without her faithful prayers? That is questionable, at best.

If you have a teen in your home or in your life, regardless of where they are in their personal commitment to Christ, if you have never released them into the care of the heavenly Father, take a moment now and offer them up to God in prayer. After you've done this, begin to treasure this trust and watch God work in their lives.

If you have offered your child to the Lord numerous times and he or she is still struggling desperately, renew your trust and embrace the Master afresh. The Lord wants you to know that "You, dear children, are from God and have overcome them, because the One who is in you is greater than the one who is in the world" (1 John 4:4).

PREPARING YOUR TEEN FOR THE NEXT SEASON

Like Mary, if you have spoken out of frustration and anxiousness to your teen, but he or she has not been able to put it into proper perspective, ask for their forgiveness. Whether forgiveness is given in return or not, continue on in your love, for the Scripture reads for you today, "This then is how we know that we belong to the truth, and how we set our hearts at rest in his presence whenever our hearts condemn us. For God is greater than our hearts, and he knows everything" (1 John 3:19,20).

Were the hearts of the mother of this confused and rebellious teen and Fanny Crosby's mother woven together with Mary's in Jerusalem that day so many years ago? In some huge way I think they were.

Luke 2:51,52 says that following this event when Jesus was 12, "Then he went down to Nazareth with them and was obedient to them. But his mother treasured all these things in her heart. And Jesus grew in wisdom and stature, and in favor with God and men." He went home and submitted to His parents and their input for 18 years.

Yes, this was the day Jesus discovered who He was. However, it was also the day He chose to demonstrate to mankind throughout the ages the importance of honoring your parents and not despising daily life, for both are seedbeds of preparation for the future.

We need to ponder the moment of release as a hidden treasure in our hearts and let our teens' knowledge of who their father is go beyond that of their earthly father to their heavenly Father.

Release, trust and treasure, for therein lies your teen's solid foundation and hope in Christ for the next season of life.

Notes
  1. Fanny J. Crosby, *Fanny J. Crosby: An Autobiography* (Grand Rapids, Mich.: Baker Book House, 1986), p. 24.
  2. Ibid., p. 22.
  3. Ibid., p. 35.
  4. Ibid., p. 44.
  5. Ibid., p. 46.

Chapter 10

RELEASING INTO ADULTHOOD

On the third day a wedding took place at Cana in Galilee. Jesus' mother was

there, and Jesus and his disciples had also been invited to the wedding. When

the wine was gone, Jesus' mother said to him, "They have no more wine."

"Dear woman, why do you involve me?" Jesus replied. "My time has not yet come."

His mother said to the servants, "Do whatever he tells you."

Nearby stood six stone water jars, the kind used by the Jews for ceremonial

washing, each holding from twenty to thirty gallons.

Jesus said to the servants, "Fill the jars with water"; so they filled them to the brim.

Then he told them, "Now draw some out and take it to the master of the banquet."

They did so, and the master of the banquet tasted the water that had been

turned into wine. He did not realize where it had come from, though the ser-

vants who had drawn the water knew. Then he called the bridegroom aside and

said, "Everyone brings out the choice wine first and then the cheaper wine after

the guests have had too much to drink; but you have saved the best till now."

This, the first of his miraculous signs, Jesus performed at Cana in Galilee. He

thus revealed his glory, and his disciples put their faith in him.

JOHN 2:1-11

To run out of wine at a wedding would be a *faux pas* long remembered in the small town of Cana. It was the kind of social blunder that could become the subject of mockery and ridicule, not only in the local neighborhood but also in neighboring towns for years to come.

This time, Mary was thankful that the women's quarters were located so close to where the wine was stored at these long wedding feasts. It allowed her to overhear the servants speaking of the need. She would not want her friends to be humiliated by a lack of wine at this wonderful wedding celebration.

Guests were supposed to help defray the costs of the wedding with their gifts, and she had not been able to bring much. Jesus and His new friends had arrived; He would know what to do. He had been such a wonderful provider for her since Joseph's death; surely He would know what to do now.

Even though Mary was older now, she was still a woman who saw a need and desired to help meet that need. She also still had a personality that sparkled with verve and determination. She was willing to barge in where others might fear to tread.

Have you ever wondered what moved Mary to ask Jesus to fix the problem at the wedding? Have you ever wondered what went through her mind that day? Perhaps her thoughts were along these lines:

Oh, dear Father, my poor friend and her husband are out of wine. You know what that means! I have never complained about our lifestyle and the way we have had to pinch pennies, but I sure would like to be able to help my friend, Lord. You know what the gossips will do with this. My friends will never live it down and the master of the banquet might lose his job!

Jesus will know what to do. There He is. "Jesus, oh Jesus, they're just about out of wine. You know what that could mean!"

What? What did You say? My mind is so full of concern, I don't think I heard You quite right. "Oh, servant! Whatever He tells you, do it."

That tone in His voice, what was that? I haven't heard that tone for years. In fact, it was 18 years ago at Passover—when Joseph and I found Him in the Temple—that I last heard that tone in His voice. What could it mean?

Yes, Father; yes, I release Him to do Your bidding.

Have you ever asked your adult children to do something for someone, but they weren't motivated to do it? Have you ever neglected to realize that your adult children may have their own ideas about how a situation should be handled, and you were surprised when they let you know it?

If you've ever had a responsible single adult child live with you for very long, you probably can identify with these questions and with Mary at the wedding in Cana. You often still have a certain amount of input in your young adult's life, especially when he or she is still living with you. At the same time, as you get accustomed to them carrying part of the adult household responsibilities, it's easy to become dependent on them in certain areas.

How long should adult children continue to do what you say, and when should you release them to do as they think they should? In other words, when do you shift from specifically directing them and transition into advising them? Your role as a parent and theirs as an adult child can be confusing at times, to say the least.

A CHANGE IN RELATIONSHIP

Cana was approximately six miles northeast of Nazareth. Mary obviously was well acquainted with the host and hostess of the wedding. Some scholars believe she may have even been related to this family. Hence, she would not have wanted them to suffer the horrible embarrassment of running out of wine.

The wedding host was responsible for providing his guests with adequate wine for seven days, but he would relegate the banquet details to a designated master of the banquet. This person was considered to be in a position of honor, and one of his primary duties was to regulate the distribution of wine. He would also monitor the wine and the guests for any incident that might ruin the party.

Usually the purest wine was served first and then wine that had been diluted with water served later in the week. To run out of wine was considered to be such a social failure that it ran the risk of damaging the family's reputation. To have this happen in a small town such as Cana, with closely knit neighboring towns, could have been devastating to the family name for years.

It is probable that Mary had been a widow for a number of years. Most likely, this meant one of two things, or both: (1) she was used to being in charge—she was used to being aware of the needs of a household and making sure those needs were met; (2) she was used to Jesus, as the firstborn son, helping to meet those needs—He must have been a very attentive son, as she obviously had complete confidence that He would know what to do about the situation.

It doesn't appear that Mary took His response as an insult or an unwillingness to meet the need, or she would not have instructed the servants to do whatever He told them to do. Even though this is an obvious moment of release between Mary and Jesus, it was not meant to be harsh. In fact, the term "woman" was the same term in which He tenderly addressed her later while on the Cross. If this was a reproof to Mary, it was a mild one and didn't wound her or hinder her from continuing to believe that He would still provide an answer for her concern. If anything, this was a mild reproof for Mary's attempt to direct His steps when it was time for Him to be hearing direction from His heavenly Father.

It's interesting to note that it was when this mother saw a need that the embarking of her son's ministry took place and the first miracle was released. Mary's perception of a need kicked into gear at exactly the same time that Jesus' first major adult transaction was to take place.

I think our heavenly Father has equipped mothers with the ability to be aware of numerous needs that surround them and their children—all for good reasons, even for divine encounters that bring release into the next season of life.

Even though Mary must have felt that Jesus' words had cut the emotional umbilical cord, so to speak, it's amazing how persistent and full of faith she remained. Some might say stubborn, but I prefer to think her seeming oversight of Jesus' statement and her continuing comment to the servants was a statement of faith. She was acting in confidence that Jesus had heard her concern and would move on it.

You could easily liken her to other Old Testament pursuers of God who didn't take no for an answer. Consider Jacob in Genesis 32:22-32 when he wrestled with the messenger of God and wouldn't let him go until he received a blessing. Moses persisted with God on behalf of the people until God made a covenant with him in Exodus 33:12—34:10. Elijah was also an example for Mary in 1 Kings 18:36-38 when he cried out, "Answer me, O LORD, answer me," and then fire fell from heaven and burned up Elijah's sacrifice. And what about Elisha in 2 Kings 4:8-37, when he beseeched God to raise the Shunammite widow's son from the dead?

Had not Mary followed her ancestors' example in asking in faith, believing that it would happen? Yes, she was demonstrating that same strong faith manifested throughout the generations of her people.

She had spoken faith, but then came the time to release. When Jesus spoke the word, she had to release Him to be the adult He was and to do as the heavenly Father told Him.

RELEASING YOUR CHILD INTO ADULTHOOD

As the dean of women at a Bible college, I've watched a lot of mothers over the years go through the releasing-into-adulthood phase. Some wait anxiously and nervously in registration lines all day. Some busy themselves by carrying boxes from home, wanting desperately to arrange their son's or daughter's dorm room, only to realize the "child" wants to do it his or her way. Some sit on the lawn just outside the men's dorms and long to march right into the rooms of their sons, whom they know are hopelessly lost when it comes to arranging a room, only to be told, "Wait outside, Mom; you're embarrassing me." Some mothers are excited with the

Most mothers go through a range of emotions as they release their children into adulthood.

prospect that college life will help their child grow up. The countenances of others reveal that the nest is empty all too soon.

Two things are sure to happen when it comes to this type of release: First, when you least expect it, your emotions will show up. Second, your emotional down times will come at different times than your best friend's. Seldom compare emotional responses with another mother's, and don't try to advise your friend about how to release her child into adulthood. Her response may be completely different from yours and vice versa.

Most mothers go through a range of emotions as they release their children into adulthood. Some mothers who enroll their young adult children into university drive away in tears; some drive away in relief. Some mothers rejoice about university but struggle with the release into marriage. Some mothers rejoice when their children take to the marriage aisle but struggle with the adventures their adult children want to take when they are single.

I had such a release myself one summer. My young adult daughter, Angie, responded to an opportunity to spend her summer doing a ministerial internship under a seasoned missionary in Cambodia. She was excited with zeal for the Lord and with the spirit of adventure burning in her heart. She and another classmate made the long journey together. Angie would stay for the summer; her classmate Jenny would stay for a year.

A feeling of release was at the forefront of my heart and my trust level was high. I had always encouraged her to do something with her singleness, not just something about it. In other words, I encouraged her to enjoy her single years and do something effective and fulfilling for the Lord before she got married. That all sounds good when you're saying it, but it's different when you're living it. However, I really meant it. She was going to be with people whom we knew to be very wise and competent, and I felt good about it.

Angie's assignments while there varied from taking language classes to teaching piano lessons, Bible studies and various other things. Although Cambodian mosquitoes seemed to be attracted to her American body, she easily adapted to the culture and the heat and humidity of the area. She also quickly developed good friendships with some other young women who were there serving from the Philippines.

One late afternoon, after being there for just a couple of weeks, the girls decided to go into town to have a nice dinner. The mode of transportation in Phnom Penh is moto-taxies, taxies that are small motorcycles. The missionary had warned Angie and Jenny to never stay out past dark because they were white Caucasians, an easy target for thieves. The Filipinas would not be as easily noticed because of their Asian faces and skin tone.

The dinner in town and fellowship with the other girls was wonderful. The time had been filled with laughter, good food and sweet fellowship. By the time they left the restaurant, it was dark outside. They all hailed taxies and each went their own direction. Angie was on a moto-taxi with one of the Filipinas, and Jenny was on another.

On a side street, six thieves stopped the taxi Angie was on. Although she could not understand what they were saying, anytime she tried to say out loud something in English or Khmer, they would tap her on the forehead and look at her in a threatening manner. When she prayed or spoke the name of Jesus out loud, it was as if they didn't even hear her supplications to the Lord. They tried to get the new camera she had attached on a shoulder strap, and when she resisted, they put a gun in her ribs. In wisdom, she released the camera. Off the other girl they took all of the jewelry except her earrings. She quickly removed those before they ripped them out of her ears.

In that moment of terror, Angie had a small sign of the Lord's ever-watchful eye. (When she was 13 years old, her father had given her a special ring to signify a covenant between the two of them with a challenge for her to maintain her moral purity prior to marriage. It represents a very special connection of love and purity between them.) Even though the thieves insisted on stealing all of the other girl's jewelry, it was as though they could not see the special covenant ring on Angie's finger. To her, this was evidence that the Lord was indeed watching over her.

The next day was Father's Day here in America. Angie phoned home early that morning and began the conversation with "Happy Father's Day, Dad. I have something to tell you...." As we both sat and listened to her story, it seemed as though a hundred colliding emotions ran through my heart and mind. I heard her say the words that she was okay, but I just wanted her back in my arms where I could embrace her and make her feel safe again like a child tucked into bed at night. I wanted to be calm and offer her courage, and yet I wanted to weep woman-to-woman as I empathetically felt the violation of her personal safety.

What should I offer this now young adult daughter—the courage to stay or an airline ticket to return? Should I tell her to be brave or to retreat? Should I chide her for not obeying the missionary more specifically or offer her comfort and understanding? Should I treat her like a teen who should return home or like an adult who should remain released?

A couple of weeks after this event, internal national turmoil began to heat up within the capital city of Phnom Penh. The two prime ministers had been enemies for years. One finally found an opportunity to stage a coup while the other one was out of the country. The military generals of the army of the prime minister who was out of the country at the time lived just down the street from where the missionaries and girls were living. There was war in the streets. It was the first time in Angie's life that she ever heard real cannon fire on the Fourth of July.

Other nations were extracting their people from the nation of Cambodia. Even her Filipina comrades had to depart at their homeland's request. Although some Americans in other parts of the nation were leaving, America had not yet officially demanded that American citizens leave the nation.

We kept in touch through computer E-mails and phone calls. Again, what should we as parents do? Should we demand that she return to our definition of safety, or should we allow her to hear our counsel and then make her own decision? Again, my emotions found their moments of calmness and questioning, fear and faith.

We prayed; she prayed; we released; she stayed. She finished her exciting adventure and truly embarked on the realities of the adult world. Today she's home, finishing her schooling and preparing for her next exciting adventure, wherever that may be. Was she dedicated to the Lord as a baby? Yes. Released as an adult? Yes, that too. Is this journey of a mother's heart an easy process? Yes and no; trusting in the heavenly Father and His canopy of protection is the safest place any child could ever be—even an adult child. Is it easy to do? Perhaps not. Is it full of abiding peace and joy? Most definitely.

My heart that summer was once again intertwined with Mary's as I said to my daughter, "Do whatever He tells you." It wasn't comfortable and it wasn't easy; but it was the wisdom of God and the safest place for her.

There is coming a day, if it has not already come, when you must release your child into adulthood. You must not hold on any longer, for your son or daughter is not a child or a teen to be molded by your daily care but rather by your daily release. Do it today and watch the miracle unfold before your very eyes.

Chapter 11

RELEASING INTO DESTINY

Near the cross of Jesus stood his mother, his mother's sister, Mary the wife of Clopas, and Mary Magdalene. When Jesus saw his mother there, and the disciple whom he loved standing nearby, he said to his mother, "Dear woman, here is your son," and to the disciple, "Here is your mother." From that time on, this disciple took her into his home.

JOHN 19:25-27

They all joined together constantly in prayer, along with the women and Mary the mother of Jesus, and with his brothers.

ACTS 1:14

Mary knew that among certain elements of the population, hostility had been growing toward her first-born son. But there were so many who loved Him, so many who had been miraculously touched by Him, that she never dreamed it would come to this. And yet, in recent days, her heart had been continuously guided back to the prophet Isaiah. Chapter 53 seemed to have been her constant meditation of late.

> *He was despised and rejected by men, a man of sorrows, and familiar with suffering. Like one from whom men hide their faces he was despised, and we esteemed him not. Surely he took up our infirmities and carried our sorrows, yet we considered him stricken by God, smitten by him, and afflicted. But he was pierced for our transgressions, he was crushed for our iniquities; the punishment that brought us peace was upon him, and by his wounds we are healed. We all, like sheep, have gone astray, each of us has turned to his own way; and the Lord has laid on him the iniquity of us all. He was oppressed and afflicted, yet he did not open his mouth; he was led like a lamb to the slaughter, and as a sheep before her shearers is silent, so he did not open his mouth* (Isa. 53:3-7).

There were no angels to prepare her heart this time. Only the voice of her firstborn son could penetrate the deep sorrow she felt. Should she go to Calvary? *Could* she go to Calvary? She must. But how could she bear to look upon His tortured body? Her mind was full, but the pain of the reality she faced numbed her thoughts.

What agony Mary must have felt that day. Not only was her Messiah taking her sins upon Him and paying the price for her redemption, but her firstborn son was dying on that cross. For her it was pain beyond pain—the first child she had carried within her womb was now dying for her sins.

Oh Father, as I walk this journey to the cross of my son—Your Son—my thoughts collide against one another. I reach for one thought to meditate on and it evaporates before I can grasp it. I reach for another to bring me reason and it eludes me as well.

Can I bear this, my soul? The psalmist's words penetrate my heart and sing my song of proclamation: "My tears have been my food day and night, while men say to me all day long, 'Where is your God?' These things I remember as I pour out my soul: how I used to go with the multitude, leading the procession to the house of God, with shouts of joy and thanksgiving among the festive throng. Why are you downcast, O my soul? Why so disturbed within me? Put your hope in God, for I will yet praise him, my Savior and my God" (Ps. 42:3-5).

Truly, Your Word has always been a comfort to me, Father. Oh, but for a word, a momentary bonding, with my son—but for a moment, Father, a brief respite.

My soul cries out to You; help me to complete my journey. Strengthen my steps; open my ears and preserve my heart. I dedicate my life to You afresh. I reach for Your hand once again; together we will go.

"Highly favored," Lord? Yes, highly favored am I.

I doubt that we can really begin to comprehend what must have gone through Mary's heart and spirit that day. But neither can any one individual grasp the emotional pain another goes through at a time of release like this.

It is abhorrent to any mother to consider the possibility of her child's death before her own. When it does happen, how does one cope?

I recently heard a news broadcast in which a married couple and their seven-year-old son were vacationing in Europe. One evening, as they were driving, some gunmen accosted them, shot at their car and attempted to force them off the road. In the harrowing process, their seven-year-old son, Nicholas, was shot while sleeping in the backseat.

After arriving at the hospital and learning that Nicholas would not survive, they made a decision to donate his organs. His kidneys were soon transplanted into the body of a young single woman who was hoping to soon be married. A year after Nicholas's death, the now young married woman gave birth to a baby boy and named him Nicholas.

The mother of the Nicholas who was killed released her son to death and chose to allow life to come out of that release. Her son lives on today through the life of this young mother and her son.

WHEN SORROWS LIKE SEA BILLOWS ROLL

In 1873, another husband and wife were traveling with their children. The husband was a Christian lawyer from Chicago, Illinois, named Horatio Spafford. He traveled with his wife and four young children to the city of New York, where he had some business to attend. Upon arriving in New York, Mr. Spafford took his wife and children to the boarding docks to put them onto the luxury liner *Ville de Havre* that was sailing to France. He planned to join them in about three or four weeks, after he finished some business in New York City.

The trip started out beautifully. But on the evening of November 21, 1873, as the *Ville de Havre* proceeded peacefully across the Atlantic Ocean, the ship was struck by another vessel, the *Lochearn*. Thirty minutes later it sank to the ocean floor with the loss of nearly all on board.

When the announcement came that the ship was sinking, Mrs. Spafford knelt with her children and prayed that they might either be saved or be willing to die if that was God's will.

A few minutes later, in the terror and confusion, three of the children were swept away by the ocean waves while she stood clutching the youngest child, a baby girl. Suddenly the baby was swept from her arms. As she reached for her, she caught the baby by her gown; but then another wave came quickly and swept her away forever. Mrs. Spafford fell unconscious and awakened later to find that she had been rescued by sailors from the *Lochearn*, but the four children were gone.

It was 10 days before the *Lochearn* arrived in Cardiff where Mrs. Spafford could send a message to her husband in New York City. He had heard of the sinking of the *Ville de Havre* and was waiting anxiously to receive word. The word came: "Saved alone." That night he paced the floor in anguish and prayed to the Lord he knew and trusted. He found that peace that surpasses all understanding (see Phil. 4:7).

Sometime later, after being reunited with his wife, he wrote the well-known hymn "It Is Well with My Soul":

> When peace, like a river, attendeth my way,
> When sorrows like sea billows roll;
> Whatever my lot, thou hast taught me to say,
> It is well, it is well with my soul.
>
> Though Satan should buffet, though trials should come;
> Let this blest assurance control;
> That Christ has regarded my helpless estate,
> And has shed his own blood for my soul.
>
> My sin—O the bliss of this glorious thought!
> My sin, not in part, but the whole,
> Is nailed to the cross and I bear it no more;
> Praise the Lord, praise the Lord, O my soul!

O Lord, haste the day when the faith shall be sight,
The clouds be rolled back as a scroll;
The trump shall resound and the Lord shall descend;
Even so—it is well with my soul.

Truly, the release Mr. and Mrs. Spafford had to make in 1873 has not been wasted throughout the generations. The message of this great hymn of the Church has been a wellspring of hope and proclamation of faith for countless people.

RELEASING A CHILD INTO ADULT LIFE CHOICES

There's another kind of release that many mothers have to make in their motherhood journeys. That's the release of an adult child into a lifestyle that goes cross-grain with almost everything they have been taught in their growing-up years.

This is an especially difficult release for a mother to make. To make a 20-year investment into a life and then have that investment literally seem for nothing almost goes beyond what the human heart can contain. The wounded mother's heart needs healing, and yet healing seems to evade the grasp unless she gives a release. This release, just like all the other types of releases, lets go of the child while holding tightly to God.

One young man's dying words to his brother were, "Tell my story wherever it may help someone." To tell his story, of course, is to tell his mother's story. She gave birth to three beautiful children, two boys and a girl. The baby girl died at birth, but the boys were strong and healthy. It was difficult to lose the life of her firstborn baby daughter; but she, like so many brave mothers before her, made a choice to focus on the blessing of life in the two children that remained.

She had come to know the Lord in a personal way, even though her husband had not, and she was determined that her sons would enjoy the blessings of the Christian life. She was faithful to attend church and was actively involved in children's ministries all the years her sons were growing up. They shared the joy and fun of having a common bond in Christ.

When it came time, the oldest son went to Bible college and then became a pastor. What he had seen in his mother's life in the way of values and her relationship with the Lord had influenced him to make the same decisions.

During this time, the younger son began to seek out friendship from others. His father was an excellent provider for the family but wasn't around enough to develop a close emotional tie with his sons. The boy longed for male companionship. His loneliness seemed to haunt his every step. When it came time to go to college, he made the decision to go to a Christian college in hope of finding true friendship.

His brother introduced him to a minister friend, not knowing of the minister's sexual weaknesses. As they developed a friendship, the minister began to sexually molest the young man. When he attempted to get help from the school leaders, they threatened to dismiss him from school rather than understand his confusion and need for counsel. He withdrew from school and began to attend another church in town with the hope of getting help. Rather than getting the kind of help he desperately needed, he was molested by a person in that church as well. At this point, he not only withdrew from school and church but from life as he knew it.

Although his mother didn't understand all that was going through her son's mind, she released him to walk the pathway of his adult choices but held closely to him through prayer.

During those young adult years, he walked away from God and the family. He started a business that began to thrive.

Seeming prosperity was all around him. He had new friends, a nice car and a flourishing business. What more could he want out of life?

His mother continued to pray for him and reach out to him as much as he would allow. He didn't have much time for her in those days; he invested himself in a friend who understood him and his needs more. Although his mother didn't understand their relationship, it didn't daunt her love for her son. She invited his friend to family dinners and fellowship times. She was willing to take in another son, if only the son of her womb would return to the family bond.

Then his business began to go down financially. It continued to slide into financial debt until he could no longer hide it from her. At his request, she jumped in with sleeves rolled up and literally almost rescued the business through working and investing a lot of money in it. To her the money was a small price to pay, for the prodigal son had returned. Her heart was rejoicing once again.

His commitment to the business was short-lived. He walked away from it, leaving the once-again failing business at her doorstep. At the same time, his relationship with his friend ended. As a result of all these things, he asked if he could move back home. He went into a deep depression and spent days at a time in bed. His mother would talk to him and encourage him. There was still so much more of life yet to be lived. She prayed for him, served him and loved him in any way that she could.

One day he could no longer endure the desperation that filled his heart; he decided to leave the safety of his home once again and return to his friends who walked a different pathway. Once again this mother was reduced to releasing him as she simultaneously held on to him in prayer.

He hadn't felt well in a while and got a physical checkup. The doctor's words came like a knife to his soul; "You are HIV-positive." When he later realized that he had full-blown AIDS and could no longer live on his own, once again he came back to the safety of his mother's arms. This time he came not with a need for an earthly rescue but with desperation in his heart to return to the God of his childhood. He came humbly, acknowledging that he had made many poor choices in life that had led him down a pathway of death. The latter part of his days were more wonderful than any of his prior adult years, as he was restored to his church family and to his heavenly Father. Though the physical battle raged, communion was precious and sweet.

His mother was there day in and day out. She loved him, prayed for him, stood by him and released him into his final destiny. How could her son's life be remembered, even though he died? Through his father, who made a decision to follow and serve the Lord that he might see his son again in heaven.

Regardless of whether it is a release to death or a release to marriage and career opportunities, all mothers will experience releasing their children into their ultimate destiny.

His life also lived on through his mother and his brother, who would embrace the message of his life and do as he requested— "tell his story wherever it may help someone."

RELEASING CHILDREN INTO THEIR ULTIMATE DESTINY

Many mothers have experienced the death or the open rebellion of a child in some way; many have not. However, all mothers will experience releasing their children into their ultimate destiny. Regardless of whether it is a release to death or a release to marriage and career opportunities, it is a separation. Just as with the other releases in the journey of motherhood, once it takes place, life will never be the same.

Last Sunday my little two-year-old nephew toddled over to me during a prayer service at church before the formal service began. I picked him up and we chatted a bit. He rested contentedly in my arms as he played with my necklace and then my earrings. What wonder, what curiosity two-year-olds have; watching them in the art of discovery is sheer pleasure.

After my arms wearied of holding him, I passed him on to my husband. It wasn't long before he toddled off to visit another aunt and uncle. As I watched him go, tears began to fill my eyes, and my arms began to ache for the joy of a grandchild to hold. To have them close and be able to see their daily charms and mannerisms develop would be such joy.

A year previous to this, my husband and I watched our son and his bride drive off to become youth pastors some 3,000 miles away from us. Today the reality of our daughter marrying someone who will take her far from us looms large on the horizon. Truly the Lord has taken me up on the dedication of my children to Him.

What joy it brings to me that both of them are serving the Lord in their generation. What emotional sacrifice it is to release them to the fulfillment of their destinies in such faraway locations. When I see others playing with their grandchildren and enjoying shopping excursions with their adult daughters and daughters-in-law, I sometimes long for things to be different. It is in those moments that my arms ache for hugs, my eyes long to see familiar smiles, and my ears long to hear sweet familial whispers. Although I appreciate the telephone and computer E-mails, they just aren't the same as a warm embrace, a shared tear or simultaneous laughter.

But it isn't long before God's gentle Spirit draws me close, and I realize that my sacrifice is "not worth comparing with the glory that will be revealed" (Rom. 8:18). I become freshly aware in that moment that a sacrifice made to the Lord is no sacrifice at all. For as the seed falls into the ground and dies to the Lord, it will be multiplied over and over again. Truly, it is a privilege to release my children to the destiny God has for them.

In moments like these I wonder if my spirit has just tapped into the heart and life of Mary. I'm thankful that Mary walked the motherhood journey ahead of me. Truly, the light of her pathway has shined on mine time and time again.

HEALING GRACE FOR MOTHERS

Most scholars agree that Jesus made seven major statements on the Cross in the midst of excruciating physical, emotional and spiritual pain and anguish. The third statement He made was directed to His mother and His beloved disciple John, recorded in John 19:26. When Jesus saw His mother there, and the disciple whom He loved standing nearby, He said to His mother, "Dear woman, here is your son," and to the disciple, "Here is your mother." From that time on, John took her into his home.

Even when He was bearing the sin of the world, Jesus was concerned about His mother's welfare. Evidently, His younger brothers were too young to take full responsibility for their mother, and He felt the need to make sure she was well cared for.

His statement to her and John revealed that part of His purpose in dying was to bring a healing grace to families. He wanted to let the world know then and for all eternity that family relationships matter in redemption.

The further fruit of this is found in the fact that she, along with the other women and disciples, went to the Upper Room and waited just as He instructed them to do. It is here in the Upper Room that we see Mary for the last time, waiting for her beloved son and the Holy Spirit He promised to send. It is here in the midst of His friends that she found herself bonded in fellowship.

As you've pondered the positive example of Mary's responses and releases in her motherhood journey, I pray that you've received a clear message that the only way to receive the grace to follow her example is through Jesus Christ, God's Son. When all is said and done, the greatest gift that you as a mother can receive from the life of Mary is not actually from her but from her son Jesus.

I hope you have enjoyed following her life and the lives of the other women found in these pages. Please know that I continue to pray for you in the same spirit the apostle Paul expressed:

> *I thank my God every time I remember you. In all my prayers for all of you, I always pray with joy because of your partnership in the gospel from the first day until now, being confident of this, that he who began a good work in you will carry it on to completion until the day of Christ Jesus. It is right for me to feel this way about all of you, since I have you in my heart* (Phil. 1:3-7).

Understand YOUR CALLING and ANOINTING

In *Woman You are Called and Anointed,* Glenda Malmin leads you to a deeper understanding of your individual call to serve the Lord. You will understand God's unique and specific calling and anointing that enables you to succeed.

You will find God's thoughts for you in *influence, prayer, overcoming, home, hospitality, grace, compassion, teamwork, friendship, faith, children, marriage and wisdom* and how it relates to your calling and anointing.

Very practical by nature, you will be inspired to address issues and attitudes that release the working of the Spirit in your life.

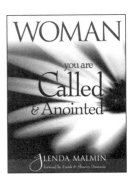

WOMAN YOU ARE
CALLED & ANOINTED
Glenda Malmin
$12.95
237 pages, Softcover

"One of the topics most on the heart of God in the church today is the ministry of women. . . Glenda Malmin has written a tender, insightful, mentoring book, which is much needed by Christian women today."
—CINDY JACOBS,
Co-Founder Generals of Intercession

Available at your local Christian bookstore
For a complete catalog of resources call City Bible Publishing 1-800-777-6057.

CITYBIBLE
PUBLISHING

www.citybiblepublishing.com